Ce Blaise Gamy

Factors associated with low birth weight

Ce Blaise Gamy

Factors associated with low birth weight

in the outskirts of Ouagadougou

ScienciaScripts

Imprint

Any brand names and product names mentioned in this book are subject to trademark, brand or patent protection and are trademarks or registered trademarks of their respective holders. The use of brand names, product names, common names, trade names, product descriptions etc. even without a particular marking in this work is in no way to be construed to mean that such names may be regarded as unrestricted in respect of trademark and brand protection legislation and could thus be used by anyone.

Cover image: www.ingimage.com

This book is a translation from the original published under ISBN 978-620-2-27450-0.

Publisher:
Sciencia Scripts
is a trademark of
Dodo Books Indian Ocean Ltd. and OmniScriptum S.R.L publishing group

120 High Road, East Finchley, London, N2 9ED, United Kingdom
Str. Armeneasca 28/1, office 1, Chisinau MD-2012, Republic of Moldova, Europe
Printed at: see last page
ISBN: 978-620-5-79831-7

SUMMARY

DEDICATION

This brief is dedicated to

to my late father Pierre Pé Minissia

and to my late adoptive mother GAALE Kolou Gnèpou Thérèse.

You have given me everything without receiving anything in return, may your souls rest in peace.

ACKNOWLEDGEMENTS

This work has been realized thanks to the contribution of several individuals and companies. We will never cease to express our gratitude to them.

To this end, I would like to express my sincere thanks to

To the International Development Research Center (IDRC), for funding my Master's degree program in Population and Health Research.

To my thesis director, Doctor Abdramane B. SOURA, for his confidence in me and who, in spite of his multiple occupations, remained always available to answer my concerns, everywhere and at any time. I would like to take this opportunity to express my deep gratitude. I would like to thank you for your rigorous scientific approach and the enthusiasm with which you have made me work. I am very pleased. May the Eternal recognize all the benefits.

To the Institut Supérieur des Sciences de la Population (ISSP), for the quality and relevance of the teaching received.

To all the professors involved in the Master in Population and Health who spare no effort in sharing their knowledge.

To BOUBA DJOURDEBBE Franklin, MILLOGO Roch Modeste and LANKOANDE Bruno, for your incessant contributions to this work. I thank you for having reassured me on certain points which seemed obscure to me, particularly within the framework of the treatment of the data base.

To all the colleagues of the ISSP office, special mention to COMPAORE Yacouba, TRAORE Harold, GANSAONRE Rabi Joël, BAGNOA Nazi Vincent, OUEDRAOGO Habibou and ZABRE Victor, for the true climate of cordial atmosphere, sharing and work that you have created around us Thank you for your collaboration.

To Madeleine ZOUNDI and Lidy TAPSOBA, for your various contributions.

To all my companions of the seventh cohort with whom, during 21 months, I shared my experiences and moments of happiness. Special mention to Dr GBEDO Sossa Edmond, you have been for me more than a brother.

Your guidance, support and advice were indeed decisive in the preparation and completion of this work.

To my dearest wife Mariam Keita and our children Lilyane Léssan and Alexandre Cé Aboubacar, for having accepted to endure certain hardships and to support me throughout this training.

To my father-in-law KEITA Aboubacar and my mother-in-law SOUMAH Léonie, for having taken care of my dear family during all this period of training. I will be eternally grateful to you.

To my dearest mother, my brothers and sisters and especially to my uncle, thank you for your support and guidance.

To all those who, from near or far, have contributed to the writing of this thesis through their advice, their encouragement and their mark of fraternity.

Finally, we would like to thank all the Guinean parents and compatriots residing or being trained here in Ouagadougou for the fraternal atmosphere that they maintained throughout our stay.

LIST OF ACRONYMS AND ABBREVIATIONS.

ACC/SCN	Administrative Committee on Coordination/Subcommittee on Nutrition
BDNT	National Territory Database
NPC	Prenatal Consultation
E & D	Children and Development
FPN	Low Birth Weight
G	Gramme
HTA	High blood pressure
IB	Bamako Initiative
BMI	Body Mass Index
INSD	National Institute of Statistics and Demography
Kg	Kilogramme
MRC/RCOG	Medical Research Council/Royal College of Obstetricians and Gynaecologists
NCHS	National Center for Health Statistics
MDG	Millennium Development Goals
WHO	World Health Organization
OPO	Population Observatory of Ouagadougou
PNS	National Health Policy
PPN	Low Birth Weight
IUGR	Intrauterine growth retardation
SPSS	Statiscal Package for Socials Sciences
UNICEF	The United Nations Children's Fund
WHO	World Health Organization

SUMMARY

Reducing neonatal and maternal mortality is one of the Millennium Development Goals (MDGs). The fight against low birth weight is one of the strategies to achieve these goals. The populations of the northern peripheral zones of Ouagadougou, which are informal, unserviced housing areas, were the targets of this study.

This was a retrospective cross-sectional study of longitudinal data collected between May 14, 2009 and May 14, 2012, with the objective of analyzing the factors associated with low birth weight in the northern periphery of Ouagadougou. It included a total of 2919 births and the characteristics of their mothers as explanatory variables.

To do this, descriptive (bivariate analysis with the cross-tabulation) and explanatory (multivariate analysis, in particular binary logistic regression) methods of analysis were used in this work.

According to the results of the analysis, the factors statistically associated with the occurrence of low birth weight in the northern periphery of Ouagadougou are: twinning, age of the mother at delivery, gestational age, ethnicity, sex and desirability of pregnancy. Factors such as the area of residence, level of education, marital status of the woman, standard of living, and activity of the mother were not statistically associated with the occurrence of low birth weight in these areas.

Low birth weight remains a reality in the northern peripheral areas of Ouagadougou and most of the factors involved can be prevented at the individual level. For this reason, emphasis should be placed on targeted and coordinated awareness-raising activities among pregnant women, their spouses and the community as strategies to reduce this phenomenon in these areas.

Key words: Low birth weight, associated factors, northern periphery of Ouagadougou.

GENERAL INTRODUCTION

The most widely used anthropometric indicator of optimal fetal weight and development[1] is birth weight (Parker *et al.,* 2001). It is an important indicator of fetal and neonatal health (WHO, 1995). Birth weight in a child is a simple way to assess the course of a pregnancy and to estimate the short-, medium-, and long-term risks to the newborn. Measured and analyzed at the population level, birth weight distribution is one of the indicators used in studies of fetal and neonatal health (ZEITLIN & BLONDEL, 2003). It also provides information on the health and nutritional status of the most vulnerable groups, namely mothers and children (CHAULIAC, 1991).

The incidence of low birth weight (LBW) reflects the health and nutritional status of pregnant women and children at a population level. It has been proposed as an indicator for monitoring health progress (WHO, 1981).

Low birth weight is a major public health problem in both developed and developing countries because of its magnitude and strong association with neonatal and infant morbidity and mortality (UNICEF, 2004). Low-weight newborns are at greater risk of dying in the first year of life and developing chronic health problems compared to those with normal weight (BDMS-ONE, 2010). It is estimated that approximately 15 million children are born underweight each year, more than one in ten births (WHO, 2012), representing 17% of all births in the developing world, a rate that is twice as high as that in developed countries (7%) (UNICEF, 2004). Similarly, there are over five million deaths worldwide each year attributable to low birth weight (WHO, 1994).

In 1995, of the 11.6 million under-five deaths in developing countries, 6.3 million (53%) were associated with low birth weight (ACC/SCN, 2000). In 2002, this figure was 3.4 million in these countries (WHO, 2002).

New statistics published in the latest WHO report illustrate both the magnitude of the problem and the presence of disparities between countries (WHO, 2012). Low birth weight is the second leading cause of death after pneumonia, and of the 11 countries[2] with rates above 15%, only two are not from sub-Saharan Africa (WHO, 2012).

Low birth weights may result primarily from either *preterm birth[3]* or *intrauterine growth*

---

1 Optimal fetal development can be defined as the state at birth that gives the newborn the greatest chance of surviving and thriving during the neonatal period and infancy and predisposes the newborn so that its initial development does not have adverse consequences later in life.
2 The 11 countries with preterm birth rates above 15% are: Botswana 15.1%, Mauritania 15.4%, Indonesia 15.5%, Pakistan 15.8%, Gabon 16.3%, Mozambique 16.4%, Equatorial Guinea 16.5%, Zimbabwe 16.6%, Comoros 16.7%, Congo 16.7% and Malawi 18.1%.
3 A premature birth is a birth that occurs before 37 weeks of amenorrhea.

retardation[4] or a combination of both (ALBANE, 2005).

The determinants of low birth weight are both multiple and complex, and they are related to different factors that can be prevented either at the individual or collective level, and some of these factors can vary in time and space (CASILLI, 2002).

The nutritional status of the woman before and during pregnancy, the physical and emotional health before and during pregnancy, environmental and intergenerational factors, the mother's medical history, the use of prenatal consultation services, maternal infections and tropical diseases, are among the elements closely incriminated in the occurrence of low birth weight, which thus directly compromise the normal development of the fetus (DAVIDSON, 1992).

These proximate factors are themselves influenced by distant factors. For example, the age of the mother at first pregnancy is largely determined by cultural and social factors. Thus, when more is invested in the education and empowerment of girls and women, the first pregnancy generally occurs later and harmful cultural factors become less important (KLEBANOFF *et al.,* 1997). The same is true for education, which can give women a greater sense of personal responsibility and distance from tradition, better access to health information and services, better financial accessibility, and greater decision-making power with respect to access to care (OUEDRAOGO, 1994).

Thus, it is not possible to act on the proximate factors of low birth weight while ignoring the distant factors, because the latter necessarily influence the proximate factors. Hence the importance of identifying the associated factors and seeking to understand the social inequalities of low birth weight.

Although studies on low birth weight exist, the results are mixed across countries, regions, and residence within countries.

Moreover, in Burkina Faso, low birth weight has been the subject of only a few studies dealing with obstetrical risk factors for low birth weight at term in rural Sahelian areas (KABORE *et al.,* 2007).

Very little of this work has been done in urban areas, particularly in a large city such as Ouagadougou, which has seen an increasing proliferation of informal settlements in recent decades as a result of urbanization, and where social inequalities are clearly observable.

Hence the importance of the choice of this work entitled "**Analysis of factors associated with low birth weight in the northern outskirts of Ouagadougou**".

Thus, based on the problems listed above in relation to low birth weight, this study aims to answer

---

4 Intrauterine growth restriction (IUGR) is a *full-term* delivery with a birth weight of less than 2500 g.

the following research question: **"What are the factors associated with low birth weight in the outskirts of Ouagadougou**? To achieve this, the following objectives were set:

General objective

The study seeks to contribute to the analysis of factors associated with low birth weight in the areas monitored by the Ouagadougou Population Observatory.

Specific Objectives:

• Identify the different factors associated with the occurrence of low birth weight in these areas monitored by the Ouagadougou Population Observatory.

• To seek explanatory elements related to the occurrence of factors associated with low birth weight in these areas.

CHAPTER I: REVIEW OF THE LITERATURE ON FACTORS ASSOCIATED WITH LOW BIRTH WEIGHT

The literature on low birth weight studies in Africa and around the world is extensive. In this study, particular attention will be paid to work that has highlighted the influence of a number of factors that may explain the occurrence of low birth weight.

In an effort to understand the interaction of these different variables, they have been classified into groups of factors that include: pregnancy-related factors, genetic and constitutional factors, demographic factors, socioeconomic factors, socio-cultural factors, diet, prenatal care, medical history, maternal infections, and lifestyle habits.

1.1 Pregnancy-related factors

1.1.1 Duration of the pregnancy

The average length of pregnancy is 40 to 41 weeks from the first day of the last menstrual period. More generally, a baby born between 37 and 42 weeks is considered to be full term, before 37 weeks, the baby that is born is said to be preterm and may be born with a low birth weight (BHUTTA *et al.,* 2005).

The length of pregnancy is a major determinant of birth weight.

Indeed, the fetus gains much of its weight in the last weeks of pregnancy. Thus, children born before the 37^e week of gestation is completed, generally have a low birth weight (EZECHI, 2003). The determinants of intrauterine growth retardation (IUGR) and low birth weight (LBW) are not the same; therefore, it is necessary to study them separately to determine the influence of each factor and its interaction (KRAMER *et al.,* 1998).

1.1.2 Type of birth

Pregnancies resulting in multiple births are at risk for low birth weight. Twins are 11 times more likely to be born at low birth weight than singletons (PAPIERNIK, 1990).

Multiple pregnancy is an important factor in explaining birth weight, and women who carry these pregnancies are more prone to high blood pressure and anemia (MILLAR, 1990). Multiple births also result in lower birth weights and generally stunted growth in later life. Also, the risks of preterm birth, perinatal death, and disease are much higher in these multiple births. These children have a different rate of intrauterine growth than children from single births (PAMBOU, 2006).

Some studies in Canada show that the use of assisted reproductive technologies such as in vitro fertilization is partly responsible for the increasing number of multiple births and therefore a portion of low birth weight (SHAH *et al.*, 2002).

1.1.3 Primiparity[5]

Primiparity is also a factor that influences birth weight. The mother's first child often has a low weight compared to subsequent children (MABIALA-BABELA, 2007). We also note that high multiparity (5 children or more) is also a determinant of low birth weight. The effect of birth order seems to be indirect, since it interacts with the mother's age at delivery. Younger mothers (under 18 years of age) are more likely to deliver their first low birth weight baby, while older mothers may be in their second or third pregnancy (BOBOSSI, 1999).

According to a study conducted in 2008 in northern Burundi by NKURUNZIZA and KANYANA on the influence of maternal age and parity on birth weight, primiparous women are 4.7 times more likely to deliver low birth weight babies than multiparous women. These authors suggest strategies to increase the age at marriage for girls and improve targeting during prenatal counseling and delivery monitoring. These strategies would help prevent the consequences of low and high birth weight on the health of the mother and child (NKURUNZIZA, 2008).

1.1.4 Gender of the baby

The relationship between the sex of the baby and its weight at birth has been highlighted by several authors. KRAMER (1987) in his review of the literature, states that the male sex has a higher birth weight and would be more protected against intrauterine growth retardation than the female sex. Similarly, KABORE *et al.* in 2007 found that the female sex was more likely to be low birth weight than the male sex. The results of the work of MEDA *et al.* in 1995 in Bobo Dioulasso on the risk factors for prematurity and intrauterine growth retardation also confirm this fact.

1.2 Demographic factors

The intergenic interval[6] .

The intergenital interval can have an impact on birth weight (OHLSSON *et al.*, 2008). When the intergenital interval is short (less than 18 months), the mother may not have had time to build up an adequate supply of nutrients and is at risk for increased stress, which may influence intrauterine growth and the risk of preterm delivery (OHLSSON *et al.*, 2008). In addition, a short intergenital interval is often associated with young age, high parity, a history of low birth weight babies, inadequate education, or membership in a minority ethnic group. On the other hand, when the intergenital interval is longer (greater than 60 months), the risk of preterm delivery and intrauterine

---

5 Primiparity is giving birth for the first time.
6 Intergenerational interval: the period of time between the birth of one child and the conception of the next.

growth restriction increases. This is an area that can be easily modified to reduce the prevalence of low birth weight babies (SHAH *et al.*, 2002).

1.3 Genetic and constitutional factors

1.3.1 The race

Black newborns are twice as likely to weigh less than 2.5 kg at birth as Caucasians (SHIONO, 1986).

Some authors have suggested that maternal age, rather than race, is the cause of this birth weight difference between blacks and whites.

Indeed, black mothers are often younger than white mothers at first birth. However, when the birth weights of mothers of different races but of the same age are compared, the previously observed weight difference still persists in all age groups. The same is true when other parameters, such as education level, are taken into account (STARFIELD, 1991).

In addition, authors such as KESSEL (1988) and COLLINS (1997) state that black individuals have a higher rate of fetal death and a higher risk of giving birth to preterm or intrauterine growth retarded children. This racial disparity in birth weight is not due to socioeconomic status. Race and socioeconomic status have independent effects on the rate of low birth weight. This may suggest the intervention of genetic factors in birth weight (PRADA, 1998).

1.3.2 The size of the mother

Maternal height is used to identify the risk of adverse pregnancy outcomes such as low birth weight. Maternal height can be used as an indicator in place of pelvic measurements and thus as a predictor of risk for obstetrical complications such as fetal-pelvic disproportion[7] or dynamic dystocia[8] (HARRISON, 1985). Some authors find that size is not a useful indicator of pregnancy outcome, as size cannot be changed by intervention. However, it appears that adolescents do grow after nutritional intervention. In addition, height is a good indicator of socioeconomic status and can identify women at nutritional risk (HARRISON, 1985). A single height measurement taken after adolescence can be used as an indicator of reproductive risk throughout a woman's life. Cut-off values for risk vary from country to country. They should be between 140 and 150 cm (NCHS, 1981).

---

7 The fetopelvic disproportion is an anomaly complicating obstetrical labor. It corresponds to an incompatibility between the dimensions of the fetus, more precisely between the cephalic diameters and the dimensions of the maternal bony pelvis, explored by radiopelvimetry. This can occur in different species. In humans, it is resolved by performing a cesarean section before labor (prevention) or during labor.
8 Dynamic dystocia is a disturbance in uterine muscle function during labor resulting in abnormal contraction and inefficient muscle dilation.

If only the mother's height is related to the baby's birth weight, at least through the transmission of a certain genetic potential. On the other hand, the fact that a woman has a small stature could limit the growth of the uterus, the placenta and the fetus. It should also be noted that maternal height is associated with age to some extent (SHAH *et al.*, 2002).

1.3.3 The mother's weight before pregnancy

Maternal pre-pregnancy weight reflects the nutrient reserves available to the woman that will eventually be available to support fetal growth. Maternal weight also reflects socioeconomic, cultural and genetic differences that must be taken into consideration (OHLSSON *et al.*, 2008).

Excessive weight that existed prior to pregnancy or was acquired during the nine months of gestation has deleterious effects on the course of pregnancy and delivery.

According to a study carried out by OUSMANE *et al.* in 2001 in Dakar, on the body mass index (which considers both the mother's weight and height) as a determinant of birth weight, a higher than normal BMI is associated with certain complications during pregnancy such as arterial hypertension, vascular complications, longer labor often requiring recourse to Caesarean section, and preeclampsia. These complications predispose to intrauterine growth retardation, premature delivery and low birth weight.

During pregnancy, the physiological changes that take place in the woman's womb require an increased supply of energy and nutrients.

A healthy, balanced diet and appropriate weight gain during pregnancy promote normal fetal growth (KRAMER *et al.*, 1998).

According to SHETTY and JAMES (1994), in poor countries, the major determinants of low birth weight due to intrauterine growth retardation are nutritional: inadequate nutritional status of the mother before conception, low height, low weight and poor nutritional status during pregnancy. Countries with high rates of low birth weight also have a high percentage of chronically energy-deficient women and a large number of malnourished children (WHO, 1997).

Maternal nutrition during pregnancy is especially important. Low weight gain during pregnancy can account for 14% of low birth weights due to intrauterine growth restriction, and this rate can be as high as 18.5% in populations with a high prevalence of low maternal height (SHETTY, 1994).

KRAMER (1987) conducted a meta-analysis of weight gain during pregnancy associated with nutrition. He found that in mothers with low initial weight, weight gain during pregnancy further reduced the risk of having a low birth weight infant. Trials have also shown that supplementation with zinc, iron and magnesium as well as protein and energy during pregnancy prevented low birth weight (DE ONIS, 1998). In a study conducted in Burkina Faso, MEDA *et al.* in 1995 found that a mother's weight of 50 kg or less was a specific risk factor for prematurity.

1.4 Socio-economic factors

1.4.1 the mother's income

The mother's income is often combined with her education and employment status. In this regard, large socioeconomic disparities in the distribution of low birth weight babies are observed (CAMARA, 1996).

A mother's income is one of the prerequisites for attending health facilities and adopting healthy dietary and hygienic conditions. It is often considered an indicator of access to health care services and facilities. According to a study conducted in Cameroon, a mother's income of less than 25,000 CFA francs is a factor significantly associated with the delivery of a low birth weight child (TIETCHE, 1998).

The literature also shows that certain factors that increase the risk of low birth weight are found together in individuals of low socioeconomic class. These include smoking, malnutrition, obstetrical complications such as hypertension, pre-eclampsia, and genital infections (BEHRMAN, 1985).

Although it is recognized that maternal risk behaviors such as smoking, poor nutrition, and lack of prenatal care vary by socioeconomic status, the mechanisms of these interactions in relation to low birth weight are poorly understood (KRAMER *et al.,* 1998).

1.4.2 The mother's job

Maternal employment or occupation is one of the most difficult risk factors to associate directly with low birth weight because there is no consensus on how one type of employment compares to another. In addition, most studies only look at paid work. However, working at home can be as, if not more, demanding than working outside the home (HANVEY, 1994). There is also another controversy about the impact of a woman's work on her pregnancy, as it would be random to quantify the effects of physical effort on gestation, as it is considered subjective and therefore difficult to measure and compare (SIMPSON, 1993).

HENRIKSEN *et al* (1994) found that working was not a risk factor for low birth weight. The authors retrospectively asked patients seen at their first visit to a Danish hospital about their occupation during their first trimester of pregnancy (up to 16^e weeks) and about their employment status up to about 30^e weeks of gestation. The relative risk of prematurity appeared to be higher among women who were unemployed than among those who were employed outside the home, and the same was true for the proportion of low birth weight babies.

However, these results should be viewed with caution, as they do not take into account the social context in which women who do not work live. Are they poorer, less educated and more socially isolated?

However, if multiple studies show that labor is not a risk factor for growth retardation, there are others that tend to show the association between physical effort and low birth weight. ALEGRE *et al* (1984) reported that babies born to mothers who worked until delivery weighed on average 200 g less than those whose mothers had stopped working one month before delivery (in the absence of obstetric pathology). Their research, based on an analysis of questionnaires completed by 1,450 women between 1979 and 1980 in Spain, identified the characteristics of the working conditions of 730 of these women and 720 women who were part of the control group.

1.4.3 Age of the mother at delivery

Considered a crucial variable in the study of demographic behaviors, maternal age has been shown to be strongly correlated with the occurrence of low birth weight (CAMARA, 1996).

The two extremes of a woman's reproductive years (under 18 years and 35 years and older) are at the greatest risk for low birth weight. When the woman is an adolescent or 35 years of age or older, this has a significant influence on the risk of delivering a low birth weight baby (TIETCHE, 1998). Although biological reasons explain the relationship between the young age of the mother[9] and intrauterine growth, it is the risk factors more present in young girls that play the greatest role. Indeed, it is recognized that young girls have a lower level of education, their socio-economic status is precarious, they consume alcohol during pregnancy, and they do not have a healthy diet (DELPISHCH *et al.*, 2005). A study conducted in 1990 among mothers aged 13 to 23 years, analyzed and evaluated their impact on primiparity and low birth weight (FRASER, 1995). The results showed that the younger the mother, the greater the risk of giving birth to a low birth weight or a premature baby. Between the ages of 13 and 17, the relative risk is 1.7 for low birth weight, whereas it is 1.9 for prematurity.

Low birth weight is also common among mothers aged 35 years and older, but the mechanisms behind this dynamic are poorly studied. The incidence of chronic diseases such as diabetes and hypertension in older women and the use of assisted reproductive methods are plausible explanations (OHLSSON *et al.*, 2008).

Pregnancy in adolescence or at an advanced age thus carries a high risk of complication for the unborn baby. This is a fairly common phenomenon that must be taken into account in the monitoring of the pregnancy.

---

9 The development of the reproductive system is not at the optimal level.

1.4.4 The mother's marital status

Maternal marital status is an important factor in health service utilization. It has a protective effect on the risk of giving birth to a low birth weight child. This effect is indirect, however, since it is the social, emotional, psychological and financial support offered by the presence of a spouse that reduces the level of stress and promotes the duration of gestation and fetal development (CONGO, 2007).

Whether a pregnant woman is in a union, divorced, or single is a factor that, combined with her income, can influence her access to prenatal care services in one way or another. Single women, in addition to low income, may face the problem of unwanted or unrecognized pregnancy by the father, resulting in abortion attempts, which may affect the birth weight of the baby (TIETCHE, 1998).

1.4.5 Level of education

Education is an important factor of social change because it gives the individual a greater sense of personal responsibility and a distancing from tradition, in contrast to the rather resigned and fatalistic attitude of the uneducated woman (CALDWELL, 1979). In addition to being a means of disseminating Western values, which sometimes lead to low offspring, the mother's education provides her with a broad social network, new reference groups, greater identification with the modern world and, finally, a greater willingness to use health services (FRIEDL, 1982).

The level of education is a characteristic closely associated with life habits. It allows access to better income and quality care (KETTERLINUS, 1990).

Education level is also associated with low birth weight, as a Canadian study found that the incidence of low birth weight babies was almost twice as high among Montreal women with low education (less than 11 years) compared to those with 13 or more years of education. In another study conducted in Quebec, the authors reported that women with little education were twice as likely to give birth to a low birth weight child compared to mothers who had attended university (COLIN, 1989).

Thus, the woman's level of education is an important dimension in the analysis of the use of medical care (MBOUP, 1999; OUEDRAOGO, 1994).

1.5 Socio-cultural factors

1.5.1 Religion

Defined as "an institutionalized system of beliefs, symbols, values and practices relating to feelings of divinity (AKOTO, 1993), religion governs the lives of the faithful in terms of both behavior and practice. The influence of religion on the use of modern medicine will depend on the group to which one belongs. The same is true for modern health behavior. Instead of supernatural causes, it replaces social healing with individual healing" (AKOTO, 1993).

It is a determinant of fertility and health care access behaviors, although the relationship is complex (CALVES, 1996).

1.5.2 The environment of residence

The environment in which a woman lives, i.e., the urban/rural type of locality in which she lives, can influence her reproductive behavior or her access to health care services (ANOH, 2002). In a study conducted in Burkina Faso, the authors show that women living in the city of Ouagadougou make the most use of medical consultations (23%) compared to an average of 20% in other cities and only 4% in rural areas (CONGO, 2007).

1.5.3 Ethnicity

Ethnicity, as a site of production of socio-cultural models with which individuals identify, is one of the important elements to take into account in the study of low birth weight and many other demographic phenomena. It influences behavioral variables such as age at first union, age at first sexual intercourse, age at first pregnancy, etc. (KOUTON, 1992).

The importance of ethnicity in the use of care during pregnancy is essentially pronounced in West Africa. In Cameroon, the first trimester of pregnancy among the ethnic groups of the Centre-South is characterized by great discretion (BENINGUISSE, 2003). The same observation was made in Burkina Faso by BONNET in 1988 among Mossi women. They consider pregnancy to be a gift from the genies. They must be discreet during the first trimester, lest the genies become angry and leave their bodies.

The influence of ethnic origin in the occurrence of low birth weight is both direct via genetics such as stature for example, and indirect via alcohol, tobacco, drug use, lower socioeconomic status (SHIONO & PATRICIA, 1995).

1.6 Prenatal care

Monitoring of the pregnancy is essential to promote the growth of the fetus.

Indeed, during medical follow-up, it is possible to detect and treat diseases or infections and to reduce or eliminate risk factors such as smoking and poor nutrition by advocating for a change in the mother's attitude. Women who do not have regular medical care during pregnancy or who attend their first prenatal visit late are likely to be young, poor, visible minorities, malnourished and smokers (SHIONO & PATRICIA, 1995).

Similarly, the consumption of iron supplements during pregnancy protects the woman from anemia because the required amount cannot be obtained by the pregnant woman through diet. The probability of delivering a low birth weight baby decreases as the maternal hemoglobin level increases. This probability is even greater if mothers do not use iron supplements during pregnancy, as mothers of low birth weight infants would have low hemoglobin levels before delivery (RIZVI, 2007).

1.7 The mother's medical and obstetrical history

The condition classically associated with intrauterine growth restriction is high blood pressure. It is estimated that a woman with hypertension is 20% more likely to have a baby weighing less than 2500 g than a woman without hypertension. In fact, any abnormality in the vascular network that can lead to decreased uteroplacental flow can cause low birth weight. Chronic lung disease, heart disease, and hemoglobin disorders also reduce the supply of oxygen to the fetus by reducing the oxygenation of maternal blood to a variable degree depending on the severity of the disease (MRC/RCOG, 1988).

The presence of uterine fibroids[10] significantly deforming the uterus is also implicated in some cases of preterm delivery. Cervico-isthmic incompetence[11] remains a classic, although not very frequent, cause of preterm birth, regardless of its own etiology (congenital or traumatic). After cervico-uterine cerclage[12] , the preterm birth rate is estimated to be around 30% in such cases (MRC/RCOG, 1988).

Concerning the history of low birth weight, JOHNSTONE and INGLIS (1974) speak of a family tendency transmitted by women, because they observe that sisters in the same line often have low birth weight babies. In a study comparing the birth weights of babies born in the same family (sisters versus sisters-in-law), they found that prematurity and low birth weight were found in the babies of women in the same family, especially when the women were related by blood rather than marriage.

1.8 Maternal infections

Some maternal infections such as bacterial vaginosis[13] , especially when bacterial strains are

---

10 A uterine fibroid is a very hard and dense mass of fibrous tissue that is part of the uterine body.

11 Cervico-isthmic incompetence: An abnormality of the cervico-isthmic zone of the uterine cervix characterized by the inability of the internal orifice of the uterine cervix, during pregnancy, to play its role as a lock (sphincter), by the traumatic destruction of its muscle fibers or by their constitutional, congenital inefficiency

12 Cervical cerclage is a surgical technique that involves placing a wire around the cervix to keep it closed until the end of the eighth month of pregnancy.

13 Vaginosis, or bacterial vaginosis, is an imbalance in the microbial flora of the vagina. It is characterized by the disappearance of lactobacilli and the multiplication of anaerobic germs such as *Gardnerella vaginalis*. It is not a sexually transmitted infection. It is rather a sign of an imbalance in the vaginal flora with the disappearance of the protective effect of Doderlein's bacillus.

involved, are thought to be directly involved in the occurrence of prematurity in up to 30% of cases (GIBBS, 1992). Other studies report a two- to three-fold increase in the risk of prematurity when vaginosis is diagnosed (MACDERMOTT, 1995).

Bacteria that are usually not very virulent, such as mycoplasma hominis and ureaplasma urealyticum, have also been implicated in some cases of preterm labor. Several authors have studied the impact of treatment of patients carrying one of these strains during pregnancy, but the results are contradictory, both in terms of preterm labor and low birth weight (LEWIS, 1995).

1.9 Behavioral factors

Certain habits of the pregnant woman can compromise the normal development of the fetus. Thus, the implications of smoking on pregnancy are numerous. There is an increase in spontaneous abortions during the first trimester, low birth weight babies, premature births etc. The mechanisms invoked are multifactorial because nicotine is a vasoconstrictor substance[14] : Through its effect on placental vasculature, nicotine reduces the utero-placental flow. In addition, carbon monoxide, by binding to hemoglobin, reduces the amount of oxygen carried by the blood.

Studies show that babies of smoking mothers can weigh up to 250 g less than babies of non-smoking mothers (JACOBSON, 1994). Since the risk of low birth weight is dependent on the dose of nicotine consumed, the weight loss is estimated at 11 g per cigarette smoked per day during pregnancy. In one publication, the authors found that the risk of having a low birth weight child increases by 1.5 for every 10 cigarettes smoked per day during pregnancy (ARMSTRONG *et al.,* 1992). In addition, the effect of smoking is more damaging when exposure to smoke occurs during the third trimester of pregnancy. Compared to normal, the weight loss for a baby whose mother is a smoker is 200 g in the last third of pregnancy, compared to 130 g in the first third. The effects of smoking during the last trimester of pregnancy are more noticeable because this is the period of maximum fetal growth (LIEBERMAN, 1994).

Passive smoking[15] is also responsible for growth retardation in newborns, but although a decrease in infant weight in mothers exposed to secondhand smoke has been observed, their exposure is more difficult to quantify (MATHAI, 1992).

It should be noted that smoking remains one of the best known factors in the pathogenesis of low birth weight. But also, it remains among the few factors on which it is possible to intervene in a less expensive way.

---

14 A vasoconstrictor is a substance that acts to constrict blood vessels. Vasoconstrictors are used clinically to increase blood pressure or locally reduce blood flow.
15 Passive smoking is the involuntary inhalation of smoke by one or more smokers in the vicinity of a person who does not smoke.

Also according to studies, a high consumption of caffeine (300 mg and more per day), may be responsible for a decrease in the baby's weight at birth but also for intrauterine growth retardation. The same study reveals that a lower consumption of caffeine (less than 300 mg per day) does not have conclusive effects on the baby's weight at birth and on its growth (HINDS, 1996).

In a study conducted in the United States, the authors revealed that 76.7% of women consumed caffeine during pregnancy. Compared to those who did not consume caffeine, women who consumed less than 150 mg of caffeine per day had a risk of 1.4 of giving birth to a low birth weight baby. This risk increases to 2.3 for those who consume doses between 151 and 300 mg. For those who consume more than 300 mg of caffeine per day, the risk is 4.6 and the decrease in the weight of the newborn in this last group is 105 g (MARTIN, 1987).

Finally, there is concern about alcohol consumption during pregnancy, as it is associated with fetal alcohol syndrome. This syndrome is responsible for intrauterine growth retardation and intellectual deficits. It is a syndrome that can be associated with prenatal and postnatal growth retardation, intellectual disability, conduct disorder and facial dysmorphism. In countries such as the United States, its incidence is estimated to be between 0.43 and 3.1 per 1000 live births (OSBORN, 1993). It is the toxicity of ethanol and its derivatives contained in alcohol on the fetus that is responsible. In addition, multiple malformations result from alcohol consumption during the periconceptional period and during embryogenesis: neurological, genitourinary, cardiac, hepatic and craniofacial (ERNHART, 1987). Authors such as STROMLAND and HELLSTROM (1996), for their part, were interested in the ophthalmic complications related to the fetal alcohol syndrome. They report anomalies of the inner chamber as well as glaucoma, cataracts, optic nerve and retinal anomalies.

Concerning the minimal dose for fetal damage, some authors such as MARBURY *et al* (1983) point out that there are no complications for the fetus when the mother-to-be consumes 15% of alcohol per week, except for the risk of placental abruption. On the other hand, VIRJI *et al* (1991) point out that among drinkers of more than two glasses per day, the incidence of babies weighing less than 2.5 kg is 33%.

MILLS *et al* (1984) report that babies born to mothers who consume more than two drinks per day weigh on average 165 g less at birth than other babies. With the consumption of one glass of alcohol per day, the risk of delivering low-weight babies is zero.

Fetal exposure to alcohol has long-term negative effects, as mothers who drink alcohol have a persistent decrease in head circumference over the years. Behavioral problems are also reportedly caused by in utero exposure to ethanol (COLES, 1993).

Researchers agree on the harmful effects of alcohol consumption during pregnancy, even if the data are sometimes different. However, alcohol, like tobacco, is one of the risk factors on which it is possible to act effectively in order to obtain tangible results.

1.10 Psychological stresses

Stress is a risk factor for the occurrence of low birth weight documented by several authors. HEDEGAARD *et al* (1993) state after their study, that there is an increase in preterm births in women under psychological stress in their last trimester of pregnancy. Although this factor is difficult to measure, other authors confirm this trend.

NORDENTOFT *et al* (1996) also evaluated the impact of psychological stressors on 2432 pregnancies and concluded that preterm labor was associated with an almost twofold increase in patients under various stresses.

Similarly, in a study by OAKLEY *et al* (1990) of 509 women with a history of low birth weight who were pregnant with their second children. These women received social support and home visits from trained midwives. As a result, the babies of mothers who received social support weighed on average 40 g more than those of other women. The experience of pregnancy and childbirth was better for the socially supported women than for the control group.

1.11 Tropical diseases

Some tropical diseases[16] , such as malaria, intestinal parasites (schistosomiasis, helminthiasis) or filariasis, considerably affect reproductive health (BOAZ, 1999).

In most endemic areas, pregnant women are the main group of adults most vulnerable to the disease. This has been studied mainly in sub-Saharan Africa, which accounts for 90% of the global burden of malaria-related disease and death (WHO, 2003). Each year, at least 30 million pregnancies occur among women living in highly endemic areas of Africa, most of whom reside in areas of relatively stable transmission. In addition, estimates show that 24 million pregnant women are at risk of malaria in Africa each year (STEKETEE, 1996).

Indeed, pregnant women are more at risk of developing a malaria infection than non-pregnant women, since pregnancy reduces the woman's immune power (BRICAIRE, 1993).

During pregnancy, this burden is attributable to *Plasmodium falciparum* which is the most common species in Africa. The effects of the other three human malaria parasites (*P. vivax, P. malaria, P. ovale*) are less clear. Malaria in Africa is estimated to be responsible for 15% of maternal anemia, 35% of "preventable" low birth weight, and 5% of neonatal deaths (WHO/UNICEF, 2003).

An association between *Plasmodium Falciparum* infection and low birth weight has been

---

16 Tropical diseases are infectious diseases that are prevalent in tropical and subtropical regions.

demonstrated and was more marked in primiparous women (MATTEELLI, 1997). From a pathophysiological point of view, the placental infection would produce a decrease in the transfer of nutrients and oxygen. In addition, malaria also contributes to low birth weight through the anemia it causes in the mother (SHULMAN, 1999).

Anemia due to intestinal parasites can also make it difficult for a pregnancy to progress. These anemias are caused by parasites transmitted mainly by ingestion of contaminated food. The three most important parasites are *Ascariasis lumbricoides, Trichuris trichura* and hookworms (STEKETEE, 2003).

Studies in Nepal among pregnant women and in Zanzibar among non-pregnant women suggest that eradication of hookworm infections in the study population could prevent 41-56% of moderate to severe anemias (STOLTZFUS, 1997).

In addition to intestinal worms, diarrheal diseases as well as respiratory infections are very common in pregnant women in tropical areas and have a great impact on intrauterine growth retardation. These conditions can reduce birth weight by at least 45 g (KRAMER, 1987).

Although this review of the literature is not exhaustive, readers were able to see that there are many risk factors associated with low birth weight. In some cases, preventive interventions can reduce the incidence of low birth weight without eliminating these risk factors (e.g., history of prematurity, health problems, etc.), while in others, interventions can eliminate or lessen the impact of risk factors. Smoking, poor nutrition, and drug and alcohol use are some examples.

1.12 Conceptual framework

In summary, the different determinants influencing birth weight are summarized in Figure 1. These determinants are grouped into the following groups of factors maternal characteristics that include behavioral factors (smoking, alcoholism), pregnancy factors (length of pregnancy, parity, type of birth, and sex of the baby), genetic factors (maternal race and height), socio-cultural factors (religion, residence and ethnicity), demographic factors (inter-generational interval), socio-economic factors (income, employment, age of mother at delivery, marital status, education) and other groups including prenatal care (medical monitoring of pregnancy and micronutrient supplementation), lifestyle (smoking, alcohol consumption and other stimulants), diet (weight before and during pregnancy), obstetric and medical factors (history of prematurity and history of intrauterine growth retardation, high blood pressure), maternal infections (vaginosis and bacterial strains) and psychological stresses.

All of these factors will affect the baby's weight either directly through malnutrition or the intergenerational cycle of malnutrition in the mother, or through the monitoring of the pregnancy, or indirectly through the weight of religious belief, cultural practices, genetics, or the health status of the mother.

The absence of medical monitoring of pregnancy and micronutrient supplementation has a retarding effect on the intrauterine growth of the fetus, thus influencing its birth weight. This lack of prenatal care can also cause the pregnant woman to be over or underweight, exposing her to either malnutrition resulting in intrauterine growth retardation or obstetrical complications[17] at the time of delivery, which are themselves influenced by stress. Prenatal care may in turn be influenced by other factors such as a woman's employment, income, or education level.

Similarly, the consumption of stimulants (such as tobacco and alcohol) by the pregnant woman can be the cause of spontaneous abortion, reflecting the weight of the baby at birth. This lifestyle habit influences the nutritional status of the pregnant woman, but conversely, it is also influenced by stress.

Finally, maternal infections such as vaginosis and bacterial strains may be the cause of prematurity and intrauterine growth retardation, but also of psychological stresses that can disrupt the normal development of the fetus and thus affect its birth weight. The treatment or neglect of these infections can depend on both socio-economic factors and the mother's level of education. All these factors disturb the health of the mother and hinder the normal development of the fetus through either intrauterine growth retardation (IUGR) or the delivery of premature babies with, in most cases, low birth weight.

We have mapped out the interactions of these different factors contributing to the occurrence of low birth weight using the following conceptual framework.

---

17 Obstetrical complications or complications of pregnancy are conditions and pathological states caused by pregnancy. We can also add diseases that existed before the pregnancy but are unbalanced by it.

Figure 2: Conceptual diagram of the determinants of low birth weight.

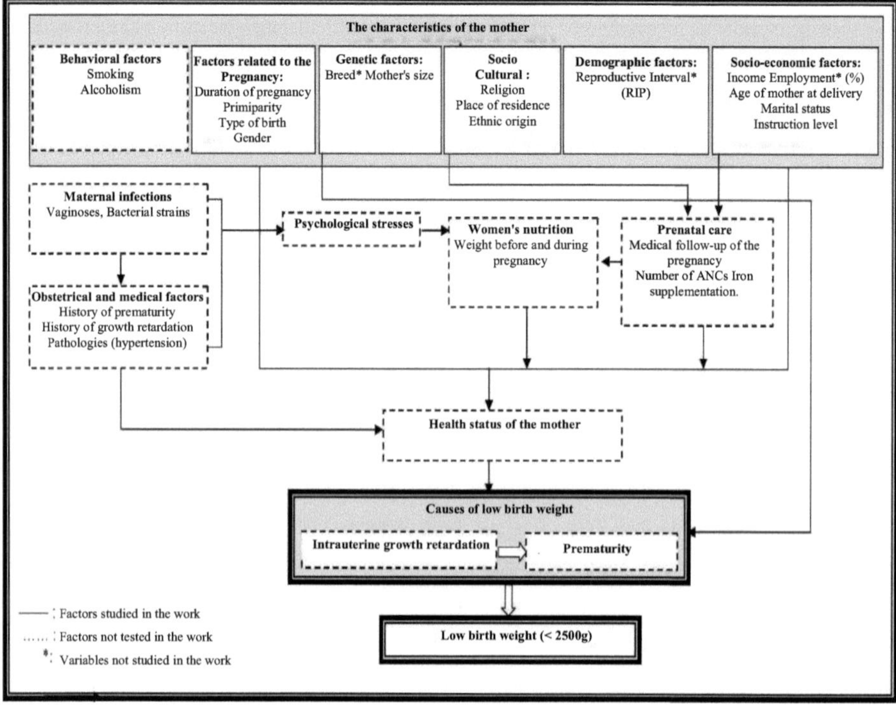

The characteristics of the mother
Behavioral factors
Smoking
Alcoholism
Factors related to the Pregnancy:
Duration of pregnancy
Primiparity
Type of birth
Gender
Genetic factors:
Breed* Mother's size
Socio Cultural :
Religion
Place of residence
Ethnic origin
Demographic factors:
Reproductive Interval*
(RIP)
Socio-economic factors:
Income Employment* (%)
Age of mother at delivery
Marital status
Instruction level
Maternal infections
Vaginoses, Bacterial strains
Psychological stresses
Women's nutrition
Weight before and during pregnancy
Prenatal care
Medical follow-up of the pregnancy
Number of ANCs Iron supplementation.
Obstetrical and medical factors
History of prematurity
History of growth retardation
Pathologies (hypertension)
Health status of the mother
Causes of low birth weight
Intrauterine growth retardation
Prematurity
Low birth weight (< 2500g)
Factors studied in the work
Factors not tested in the work
*: Variables not studied in the work

I.12 Research hypothesis

Based on the literature review and the conceptual framework, the main hypothesis of this study is that pregnancy-related factors (such as length of pregnancy, type of birth, sex of the child) and demographic factors (age of mothers at delivery, marital status) are more important than sociocultural and economic factors in explaining the occurrence of low birth weight. Based on this main hypothesis, specific hypotheses about the relationships between the different explanatory variables and birth weight were formulated. Table 1 summarizes the commonly accepted relationships as well as the hypotheses formulated.

Table 1: Synthesis of hypotheses on the meaning of relationships.

Features	Commonly accepted relationships	Hypotheses on the meaning of the relationship
Gestational age	A full-term pregnancy is 37-42 weeks. Any birth before 37 weeks is considered premature and the weight is likely to be less than the normal 2,500kg.	Preterm births are more prone to low birth weight than full-term births.
Twinning	Twin pregnancies are considered to be more prone to hypertension and anemia, which are factors that interfere with the normal development of the fetus.	Twin pregnancies are more prone to low birth weight than single fetal pregnancies.
Age of mothers at delivery	Mothers under 20 years of age and those 35 years of age and older are more at risk of low birth weight. This is due to the low level of education and the immaturity of the organism in some, and the frequency of coronary diseases and the use of assisted reproduction methods in others.	Mothers under 20 years of age and those 35 years of age and older are at greater risk of low birth weight than those between 20 and 34 years of age.
Marital status	Low birth weight is more common among unmarried women than among those in union, because of their reduced economic power. They make less use	Women outside of unions are more likely to have low birth weights than those in unions.

	of ANC services.	
Desirability of pregnancy	Unintended pregnancies are often the subject of non-maintenance and late referral to ANC services, which puts the baby's life at risk.	Mothers carrying unwanted pregnancies are at greater risk of low birth weight than those carrying wanted pregnancies.
Types of zones	The unsettled areas of large cities are more disadvantaged in terms of access to health services and pregnant women living there do not seek ANC services.	Women living in unsettled areas are more at risk of PNF than those living in settled areas because of the lack of health infrastructure.
Level of education	Women with less education are unaware of the scope of PNC and are therefore more prone to PNF.	Having no education is a factor associated with PNF, as these women are often unaware of the importance of ANC.
Gender of the child	Female babies are more susceptible to maternal malnutrition in the womb than male babies. This fact is rooted in their genetic makeup.	Females are more likely to be underweight than males because of their greater susceptibility to intrauterine growth restriction.
Household standard of living	Low-income households have low financial means and this limits their use of care services	LBW is more common among mothers from low-income households than among those from high-income households.
Activity carried out	Physical labor results in the production of kilocalories which, when not corrected by good nutrition, exposes the life of the newborn.	Working for pay is a protective factor against LBW.
Ethnic group	The cultural beliefs and practices of Mossi women prohibit early declaration of pregnancy, which implies late access to ANC services.	Mossi women are more exposed to NPF because of their cultural beliefs and practices than other non-Mossi women.

CHAPTER II: STUDY CONTEXT AND METHODOLOGICAL APPROACH

In this second part of the study, we will describe the social and health context of the city of Ouagadougou and the northern peripheral districts, and the methodological approach used throughout the study. But also, the description of the study environment, the operationalization of the different variables studied, the description of the analysis methods used as well as the description of the sample used for the analysis.

11.1 Socio-sanitary context of the city of Ouagadougou and its peripheral districts

The city of Ouagadougou, the capital of Burkina Faso, has experienced vertiginous growth since the early 1980s. This growth has been reflected both spatially by the expansion of the city and demographically by the increase in the number of city dwellers (KAFANDO, 2004).

Today, it accounts for 10% of the population of Burkina Faso and has one of the highest rates of urban growth in West Africa, which can be explained by a strong rural exodus, in addition to the return to the country of many Burkinabe expatriates following the Ivorian crisis. This phenomenon has resulted in the expansion of so-called "undeveloped" areas with high population densities (1/3 of the population of the capital) living in precarious and unhealthy housing conditions without access to basic social services (E & D, 2011).

With a population of 1.4 million in 2006, the municipality of Ouagadougou covers an area of 52,000 hectares, of which 21,750 are urbanized. It is a commune with special status comprising five (12) arrondissements[18] , 55 sectors in total (INSD, 2009).

Health indicators for children are not very satisfactory. Over the 10-year period preceding the 2003 DHS, under-five mortality was estimated at 119 deaths per 1,000 births (INSD, 2004). This is one of the highest mortality levels in African capitals. The proportion of underweight children under 5 years of age is 17.5 percent, the prevalence of acute respiratory infections in children under 5 years of age is 23.5 percent, the infant mortality rate is 69 percent, and the child mortality rate is 119 percent.

In terms of nutrition, the proportion of underweight children in Ouagadougou in 2003 was 17.5

---

18 The districts of the commune of Ouagadougou: district No1: includes sectors 1 to 16; district No2: includes sectors 7, 8, 9, 10 and 11; district No3: includes sectors 12, 13, 14, 15 and 16; district N4: includes sectors 17, 18, 19 and 20; district N5: includes sectors 21, 22, 23 and 24; district N6: Includes areas 26,27,28 and 29; Borough N7: Includes areas 30, 31, 32 and 33; Borough N8: Includes areas 34, 35 and 36; Borough N9: Includes areas 37, 38, 39 and 40; Borough N10: Includes areas 41, 42, 43, 44 and 45; Borough N11: Includes areas 46, 47, 48 49, 50 and 51; Borough N12: Includes areas 52, 53, 54 and 55.

percent, compared to 20.5 percent for the urban area as a whole and 40.3 percent for the rural area; the proportion of births with a minimum of four prenatal visits was only 39 percent (DHS, 2003).

This poor health status reflects the crises that the country is going through, including unemployment, poverty, poor housing conditions and public hygiene, which have increased in certain neighborhoods and informal settlements in the city of Ouagadougou as a result of accelerated population growth and urbanization (INSD, 2004).

In these areas, the annual growth rate (4.1%) is close to that of the city of Ouagadougou (4.2%). The population of this area has grown at a rate of 6.2% in less than two years. Net migration is positive and corresponds to an increase of 3.5% in the population. The natural balance (births - deaths) is also positive with an increase of 2.8% of the population. This growth is partly due to immigration (56%), and partly to natural increase (44%). (ROSSIER *et al.*, 2011).

In these areas monitored by the Population Observatory, we have two types of residence: a serviced area (serviced) and an unserviced area (unserviced). In terms of health, in the undeveloped areas, infant mortality is higher (28%) than in the developed areas (19%), as is juvenile mortality (8% in the undeveloped areas compared to 4% in the developed areas).

There are more women in unions (42%) than men (39%). The population is younger in the non-allocated area: 42% are under 15 years of age (compared to 36% in the allocated area) and only 5% are 50 years of age or older (compared to 8% in the allocated area). 91% of these residents belong to the Mossi ethnic group and none of the other ethnic groups exceeds 2% (ROSSIER *et al.*, 2011).

The greatest concentration of urban poverty is found in the undeveloped areas, with significant disparities. The precarious housing conditions, promiscuity, the absence of a road system and waste treatment, the poor availability of drinking water as well as the practice of certain economic activities of survival by children (garbage digging) thus generate important health problems (E & D, 2011).

11.2 Presentation of the Population Observatory of Ouagadougou

Initiated by the Institut Supérieur des Sciences de la Population (ISSP) of the University of Ouagadougou in 2008, the Ouagadougou Population Observatory (OPO) aims to understand the various problems of the poorest urban residents, and to test innovative programs to promote the well-being of this population (ROSSIER *et al.*, 2011).

It is thus used to study health inequalities through surveys on typhoid fevers, the measurement of drinking water quality in informal areas, the link between fertility and schooling, etc.

The Observatory has received financial support from the British Wellcome Trust Foundation and scientific support from a network of national, African and international partners, including: the Institut de Recherche en Science de la Santé (IRSS) in Burkina Faso, the Institut National d'Etudes Démographiques (INED) and the Institut de Recherche pour le Développement (IRD) in France, the Université Catholique de Louvain in Belgium, the University of College London in the United Kingdom, the University of Montreal and the University of Ottawa in Canada, and the Population Council in the United States. It offers these partner institutions a set of services (Demographic Surveillance, panel, cross-sectional surveys, databases, geographic information systems, etc.) that allow them to test development projects in a defined area (OPO, 2009).

The Observatory is also a member of the international network INDEPTH[19] which gathers 34 Observatories of the same kind located in 19 countries of Africa, Asia, Latin America and Oceania. It represents the 2^e urban Observatory in Africa after the one in Nairobi, Kenya, most of the Observatories being implemented in rural areas.

It is intended to be a platform for research, multisectoral actions and interventions aimed at informing the thinking of decision-makers in order to promote cost-effective social and health programs adapted to the needs of the population, particularly the poorest. It provides policymakers, researchers, and the public with reliable, harmonized, and regularly updated data and analysis on health, education, housing, and poverty to inform their policy, strategy, and programmatic choices in these different areas for development (OPO, 2009).

The Observatory has surveyors who collect information at intervals of about 8 months. These agents regularly visit the households surveyed to collect information on pregnancies and births as well as on the characteristics of the mothers (OPO, 2009).

The population monitored is approximately 80,000 individuals divided between two "serviced" neighborhoods: Kiliwin and Tanghin; and three "un-serviced" informal settlements: Nonghin, Polesgo, and Nioko 2: Nonghin, Polesgo, Nioko 2. These peripheral neighborhoods are located in the northern part of the city of Ouagadougou and are divided between the health districts of Sig-Noghin and Kossodo. They cover an area of 65 km^2 and are home to 33.5% of the population of Ouagadougou (BOYER, 2009).

Map 1 below shows the five neighborhoods monitored by the Ouagadougou Population Observatory.

---

19 INDEPTH: The International Network for Continious Demographic Evaluation of Populations and Their Health in Developing Countries.

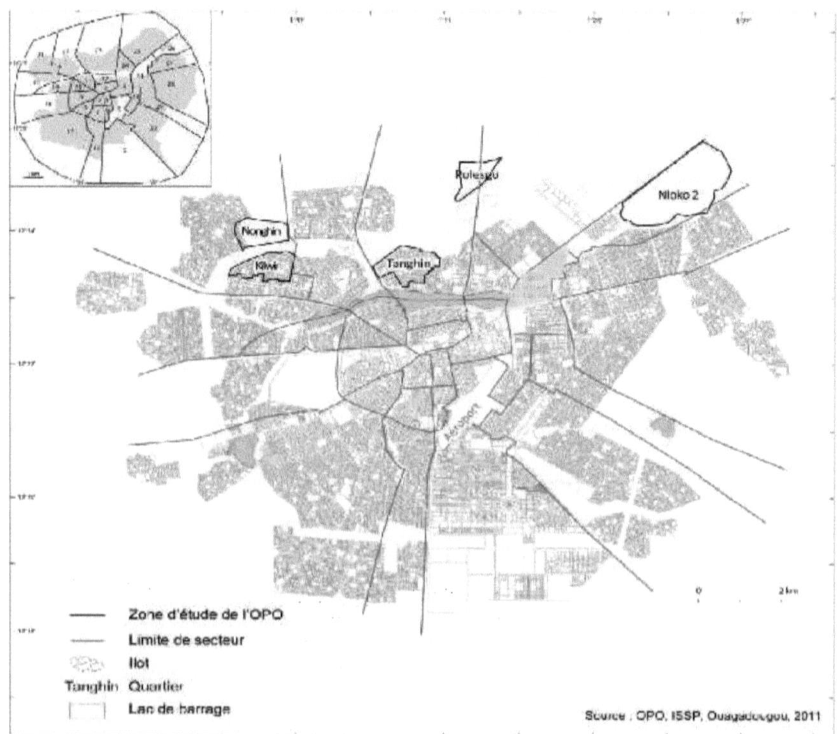

Map 1: Location of OPO areas

11.3 Type and study population

This is a quantitative cross-sectional study that is both descriptive and analytical, using longitudinal data from the database of the Population Observatory of the city of Ouagadougou. It exhaustively examined 2919 births registered between passages 1, 2 and 3 by OPO investigators (May 14, 2009- May 14, 2012).

11.4 Operationalization of the study variables

11.4.1 The dependent variable

Low birth weight is the dependent variable in this study. Taking into account the standards of the World Health Organization (WHO), a birth weight is said to be low when it is strictly less than 2.5 kg. Thus, birth weight was grouped into two categories: "low" and "normal" weight.

11.4.2 Explanatory variables

For this study, several explanatory variables were selected. For the purposes of the study, these different variables were recoded and grouped into modalities, taking into account the number of people in the initial modalities. These variables are, among others:

11.4.2.1 Age of the mother at delivery

The variable age of the mother at delivery was grouped into three age classes: those under 20 years of age, those between 20 and 34 years of age, and those 35 years of age and older.

11.4.2.2 Type of housing area

This study focuses on populations living in five different neighborhoods (2 developed neighborhoods and 3 non-developed neighborhoods). This variable was therefore grouped into two modalities: the developed area and the non-developed area.

11.4.2.3 Twinning

This variable was grouped into two modalities: babies from a singleton pregnancy (one child at birth) and babies from multiple pregnancies (2 or 3 children at birth).

11.4.2.4 The mother's marital status

The mother's marital status variable used in this study was grouped into two modalities, namely those who are married and those who are not married (single, divorced, and widowed).

11.4.2.5 The level of education

In order to assess the mother's level of education in the occurrence of low birth weight in this work, this variable was grouped into three modalities namely: those with no education, those with primary education and those with secondary education and above.

11.4.2.6 Desirability of pregnancy

This variable was grouped into three modalities: those who wanted pregnancy now, those who wanted it later, and others.

11.4.2.7 Gestational age

The gestational age variable was grouped into two modalities: babies born before 37^e weeks qualified in this study as "preterm births" and those born between 37^e weeks and more qualified as "full-term births."

11.4.2.8 Household standard of living

This variable is a key determinant of accessibility to prenatal care services. It has been grouped into three modalities, namely "low" standard of living, "medium" standard of living and "high" standard of living.

11.4.2.9 The activity carried out by the mother.

This variable was grouped into three modalities: those with no activity, those with wage activity, and those with other types of activity.

11.4.2.10 Mother's ethnic group.

The mother's ethnicity was grouped into 2 modalities, namely Mossi ethnicity and the other[20] ethnic groups.

11.4.2.11 The religion of the mother

The mother's religion variable was grouped into three modalities: those practicing the Catholic religion, those practicing the Muslim religion, and those practicing other religions (such as the Protestant religion, the traditional religion, and those who reported having no religion).

11.4.2.12 The sex of the baby

It is a dichotomous variable distinguishing boys from girls.

Table 2: Summary of variables used in the study

Variable titles	Terms and conditions
Birth weight	Low birth weight Normal weight
Type of zone	Lotie Not allocated
Level of education	No Primary High school and up
Twinning	A child Two or more children
Marital status	Brides Other unmarried
Desirability of pregnancy	Now Later Other
Age of mother at delivery	< to 20 years Between 20 and 34 years old Between 35 years and older
Ethnic group	Mossi Other ethnic groups
Gestational age	Preterm births

---

20 We have grouped the following ethnic groups in the other non-Mossi ethnic groups: Bobo, Dioula, Foulani, Gourmantché, Gourounsi, Lobi, Senoufo, Touareg/Bella, Bissa, Samo and those who answered. that they did not know.

	Full-term births
Standard of living	Low Medium High
Activities carried out	No job Salaried employees Other activities
Mother's religion	Catholic Muslim Other religions
Gender of the baby	Male Female

11.5 Description of the study sample

Table 3 presents the structure of the sample used for this study and by women's characteristics. It records the numbers and percentages of the number of women included in the study and according to the terms of the explanatory variables.

Table 3: Description of the Women's Sample, OPO 2009-2012

Explanatory variables/Women Modalities_.	Workforce	Percentages (%)
Type of zone		
Lotie	1059	36,3
Not allocated	1860	63,7
Level of education		
No level	1035	35,5
Primary	1030	35,3
High school and up	854	29,3
Twinning		
A child	2805	96,1
Two or more children	114	3,9
Marital status		
Brides	957	32,8
Other unmarried	1962	67,2
Desirability of pregnancy		
Now	2562	87,8
Later on	214	7,3
Other	243	4,9
Age of mother at delivery		
< to 20 years	267	9,1
Between 20 and 34 years old	2342	80,2
Between 35 years and older	310	10,6
Ethnic group		
Mossis	2602	89,1
Other ethnic groups	317	10,9

Gestational age		
Preterm births	782	26,8
Full-term births	2137	73,2
Household standard of living		
Bottom	1570	53,8
Medium	1162	39,8
High	187	6,4
Activity carried out		
No	1813	62,1
Employees	392	13,4
Other	714	24,5
Mother's religion		
Catholic	803	27,5
Muslim woman	1915	65,6
Other religions	201	6,9
Gender of the baby		
Male	1440	49,3
Female	1479	50,7
Set	**2919**	**100 %**

Looking at the different characteristics of the mothers, it is clear that the sample shows a predominance of mothers living in non-housed areas (63.7%), and 96.1% of them carried a single-fetus pregnancy. Those who had wanted pregnancies represented 87.8%, and 67.2% of these women were not in union. Similarly, the majority of these women were between 20 and 34 years of age (80.2%), 89.1% of them belonged to the Mossi ethnic group and 73.2% had given birth at full term. Women with a low standard of living were in the majority (53.8%), 62.1% of these women were not employed, 65.6% belonged to the Muslim religion, and 50.7% of the women had given birth to female babies.

11.6 Methods of analysis

Several statistical methods were used to test the previously stated hypotheses. The data were analyzed using SPSS (Statistical Package for Social Science) version 20. The analysis began with a flat sort of each of the variables in order to assess the distribution of the different variables. Thus, the modalities with the lowest numbers were systematically grouped and recoded before presenting a descriptive table of the sample.

Then at the bivariate level, the influence of the crude effects of the explanatory factors for low birth weight was examined using a contingency table. This allowed the statistical relationships to be investigated based on assumptions about the direction of the relationship between the dependent variable and each independent variable. The significance of the association was measured using specific association tests including Chi-square and Cramer's V to assess the strength of the relationship. A statistical significance level of 0.1 (10%) was used.

While the descriptive analysis conducted in this study suggested statistical relationships between the dependent variable and some of the independent variables, these observed relationships may be spurious because they do not take into account the effects of other variables that may disrupt the relationship. It was therefore necessary to consider all variables in a multivariate approach.

This multivariate explanatory analysis was conducted using binary logistic regression because of the qualitative and dichotomous nature of the dependent variable.

Logistic regression makes it possible to identify the relationships between the occurrence of an event and each of the associated factors while controlling for confounding factors. It allows to detect interactions and to take them into account.

It also has the advantage of providing the effect of the modalities of each of the explanatory variables in the presence of the others, and finally, it will allow us to give an opinion on the different working hypotheses previously stated in the theoretical part of the study.

In the gross model, each variable was entered one by one to determine the respective effects. For the net effect, two models were selected and the variables were introduced by group of factors according to the assumptions made in the work for the first model, and then all the variables were introduced at once in the last model in order to assess the evolution of the R-two and the variation of each of the introduced variables.

CHAPTER III: PRESENTATION OF RESULTS

This chapter reports on the results of the study of factors associated with low birth weight. It will allow readers to verify whether the main risk factors identified influence low birth weight. This chapter also presents the results of the descriptive and logistic regression analyses performed.

III.1 Results of the bivariate analysis

After a presentation of the context of the study, theoretical considerations related to the explanatory factors of low birth weight, the hypotheses of the study and the methodology, we now turn to the part of the analyses devoted to the descriptive analysis. As already mentioned, in the bivariate descriptive analysis, the associations between the explanatory variables and the dependent variable (low birth weight) as well as the intensity of these associations will be examined using the Chi-square and Cramer's V tests.

Table 4: Results of the bivariate analysis

Explanatory variables / Modalities	Low birth weight		Results of statistical tests	
	Workforce	Prevalences (%)	Chi-square values and significance	Values and significances V of cramer
Type of zone			**0,012**	**0,002**
Loti	138	13,0		
Non-settled	245	13,2		
Level of education			**0,883**	**0,017**
No	141	13,6		
Primary	127	12,3		
High school and up	115	13,5		
Twinning			**269.776******	**0,304******
A child	310	11,1		
Two or more children	73	64,0		
Marital status			**0,781**	**0,016**
Brides	118	12,3		
Other unmarried	265	13,5		
Desirability of pregnancy			**4,358**	**0,039**
Now	327	12,8		
Later on	38	17,8		
Other	18	12,6		
Age of mother at delivery			**13,393***	**0,068***
< to 20 years	54	20,2		
Between 20 and 34 years old	294	12,6		
Between 35 years and older	35	11,3		

Ethnic group			3,484*	0,035*
Mossis	352	13,5		
Other ethnic groups	31	9,8		
Gestational age			3,631*	0,035*
Preterm births	118	15,1		
Full-term births	265	12,4		
Household standard of living			0,458	0,013
Bottom	208	13,2		
Medium	148	12,7		
High	27	14,4		
Activity carried out			0,271	0,010
No	237	13,1		
Employees	49	12,5		
Other	97	13,6		
Mother's religion			0,982	0,018
Catholic	109	13,6		
Muslim woman	252	13,2		
Other religions	22	10,9		
Gender			8,727***	0,055***
Male	162	11,2		
Female	221	14,9		

Note: *: significant at 10%; **: significant at 5%.

: significant at 1%; *: significant at 1‰

With regard to the results of the previous table, the statistical association tests carried out show a significant relationship between certain explanatory variables and the occurrence of low birth weight, but an absence of relationship between other explanatory variables and low birth weight is also observed.

For ease of interpretation and understanding of these results, they have been grouped as follows: Relationships present and going in the expected direction, relationships present and going in the unexpected direction, relationships absent and going in the expected direction, relationships absent going in the unexpected direction, and relationships totally absent.

111.1.1 Interpretation of the results of the association tests of the bivariate analysis.

111.1.1.1 Statistical relationships present and moving in the expected direction.

The results of our analysis show that there is a positive relationship between twinhood and the occurrence of low birth weight. The proportion of low birth weight babies is higher in mothers who give birth to twin pregnancies (64%) than in those who give birth to singletons or mono-fetal pregnancies (11.1%), and this relationship is statistically positive and significant at the 1% level.

Similarly, the analysis revealed a significant association at the 1% level between the mother's age at delivery and the occurrence of low birth weight. Among mothers whose age at delivery was less than 20 years, the proportion of low-birth-weight babies was 20.2%, compared with 11.3% for those aged 35 years and older.

With regard to gestational age, the results of the association tests show the existence of a weak positive relationship between the duration of pregnancy and the occurrence of low birth weight with a significance below the 10% threshold. The proportion of low birth weight babies is higher in preterm births 15.1% than in full term births 12.4%.

As for the sex of the baby, the results of the analysis reveal that it is strongly associated with the occurrence of low birth weight at the 1% threshold. 14.9% of female babies had a higher proportion of low birth weight than male babies (11.2%).

Finally, the analysis revealed a positive statistical association at the less than 10% significance level between the ethnicity of the mothers and the occurrence of low birth weight.

The proportion of low birth weight among mothers belonging to Mossi ethnic groups is higher (13.5%) than among other non-Mossi ethnic groups (9.8%).

111.1.1.2   Statistical relationships present and moving in the unexpected direction

It should be noted that in this descriptive analysis, none of the positive results obtained were unexpectedly consistent with the assumptions made at the beginning of this work.

111.1.1.3   Statistical relationships absent but in the expected direction.

The activity performed by the woman in this labor does not influence the occurrence of low birth weight. This relationship is statistically absent and the analysis of proportions does not show any significant difference. The proportion of women with no activity was 13.1%, compared to 12.5% for employees and 13.6% for others.

111.1.1.4   Absent statistical relationships in the unexpected direction.

Housing area was not a factor statistically associated with the occurrence of low birth weight in this work.

In fact, according to the results of the cross-tabulation, there is no significant difference between the proportion of low birth weight children among women living in non-housed areas 13.2% and those living in housed areas 13%.

Similarly, a woman's level of education is not statistically associated with the occurrence of low birth weight. When proportions are taken into account, the analysis reveals that women with no education and those with a high school education or higher all occupy proportions around 13%.

The marital status of the woman, contrary to the hypothesis, is not statistically associated with the occurrence of low birth weight in this study. The proportion of low birth weight among married women was 12.3% compared with 13.5% among other unmarried women.

Finally, the descriptive results of this study showed that whether or not a woman wanted a pregnancy was not a factor associated with low birth weight. However, taking into account the proportions, those who want to become pregnant later seem to be at greater risk of low birth weight (17.8%) than those who want to become pregnant now and the other women (12%).

111.1.1.5 Statistically absent relationships

The descriptive analysis performed in this study shows the absence of statistical relationships between the occurrence of low birth weight and the mother's religion.

In fact, the Catholic and Muslim religions occupy proportions of 13% despite the fact that the number of Muslim women is twice as high as that of Catholics (252 versus 109).

111.2 Results of the multivariate analyses

Table 5: Crude effects of binary logistic regression, OPO 2009-2012

Explanatory variables / Modalities	Low birth weight
	Gross effects
	OR values and significance
Type of zone	
Loti	Reference
Non-settled	1,01
Level of education	
No	Reference
Primary	0,892
High school and up	0,987
Twinning	
A child	Reference
Two or more children	14,33****
Marital status	
Brides	Reference
Other unmarried	1,11
Desirability of pregnancy	
Now	Reference
Later on	1,476**
Other	0,984
Age of mother at delivery	
< to 20 years	1,766***
Between 20 and 34 years old	Reference

Between 35 years and older	0,887
Ethnic groups	
Mossis	1,443*
Other ethnic groups	Reference
Gestational age	
Preterm births	1,255*
Full-term births	Reference
Standard of living	
Bottom	0,905
Medium	0,865
High	Reference
Activity carried out	
No	0,957
Employees	0,909
Other	Reference
Mother's religion	
Catholic	1,278
Muslim woman	1,233
Other religion	Reference
Gender	
Male	Reference
Female	1,386***

Note: *: significant at 10%; **: significant at 5%.

: significant at 1%; *: significant at *1%%*.

111.2.1 Interpretation of the binary logistic regression raw effects results.

111.2.1.1 Statistical relationships present and in the expected direction.

This analysis shows that there is a statistically positive relationship between twinhood and the occurrence of low birth weight at the 1% level of significance.

In fact, women who give birth to twin pregnancies are 14 times more likely to give birth to low birth weight babies than those who give birth to singleton pregnancies.

Similarly, the results of the analysis reveal that the mother's age at delivery is statistically associated with the occurrence of low birth weight at the 10% significance level. Women whose age at delivery is less than 20 years are 1.8 times more likely to give birth to low birth weight babies than those whose age is between 20 and 34 years.

Also the gestational age of the mother is statistically associated with the explanation of the occurrence of low birth weight at the 10% significance level. Women who deliver preterm births are 1.3 times more likely to deliver low birth weight babies than those who deliver at term.

In contrast to the result of the descriptive analysis, pregnancy desirability is associated with the explanation of low birth weight occurrence in the crude effect of the multivariate analysis. This association is significant at the 5% level. The risk of delivering a low birth weight baby is 1.5 times higher among those who desire to become pregnant later than those who desire it now.

The results of the multivariate analysis, as well as those of the descriptive analysis, indicate that the sex of the child is statistically associated with the occurrence of low birth weight, and this association is significant at the 10% threshold. Thus, girls are 1.4 times more likely to be born at low birth weight than boys.

Finally, ethnicity was associated with the occurrence of low birth weight in this study. The association was statistically significant at the 10% level. Women from the Mossi ethnic group were 1.4 times more likely to give birth to low birth weight babies than those from other ethnic groups.

111.2.1.2   Statistical relationships absent but in the expected direction

The study shows that being employed or not being employed has no influence in explaining the occurrence of low birth weight.

111.2.1.3   Absent statistical relationships in the unexpected direction

The results of the analysis show that there is no association between low birth weight and a number of variables including the woman's area of residence, education level, standard of living and marital status. Contrary to what was stated in the hypotheses, these variables are not statistically significant.

111.2.1.4   Totally absent relationships

As found in the results of the descriptive analysis, there was a complete lack of association between the occurrence of low birth weight and the mother's religious affiliation according to the crude effect results.

Table 6: Presentation of Net Effects

Variables and modalities	Models	
	Model 1	Model 2
Gestational age		
Preterm births	1,25* 1	1,25*
Full-term births		1
Twinning		
A child		1
Two or more children	1 15,31***	15,57***
Age of mother at delivery		
< to 20 years	2,12***	2 09***

	Model 1	Model 2
Between 20 and 34 years old	1 0,86	1 0,85
Between 35 years and older		
Marital status		
Brides	1	1
Other unmarried	1,07	1,08
Baby sex		
Female	1,35**	1,34**
Male	1	1
Mother's religion		
Catholic		0,84
Muslim woman		0,96
Other religion		1
Type of zone		
Loti		1 0,99
Non-settled		
Level of education		
No		0,84
Primary		0,96
High school and up		1
Desirability of pregnancy		
Now Later Other		1 1,29 0,94
Household standard of living		
Low Medium High		0,87
		0,84
		1
Ethnic group		
Mossis		1,24
Other ethnic groups		1
Activity carried out		
No		1,02 0,91
Employees		1
Other		**0,127**
R-two of the model	0,122	

Note: *: significant at 10%; **: significant at 5%.

*** : significant at 1%; **** : significant at 1‰

III.3 Interpretation of the results of the two net effect models

111.3.1 Model 1: Pregnancy and Demographic Factors

Model 1 relates pregnancy-related factors (length of pregnancy, type of birth, and sex of baby) and demographic factors (age of mother at delivery and marital status) in explaining the occurrence of low birth weight. It confirms that these two factors are 12.2% involved in explaining the occurrence of low birth weight.

However, marital status does not explain the difference in birth weight observed in this model. However, gestational age, twinhood, mother's age at delivery and baby's sex are variables associated with the occurrence of low birth weight in this model.

Model 2: The set of variables taken into account

This model takes into account all the explanatory variables. It confirms that marital status, mother's religion, type of residential area, level of education, standard of living, and mother's occupation are not explanatory factors for low birth weight. On the other hand, gestational age, twinhood, the mother's age under 20 years at the time of delivery and the child's sex are explanatory factors for the occurrence of low birth weight. Regarding pregnancy desirability and ethnic group, the statistical association observed in the crude effect between those who did not want to be pregnant now and low birth weight disappeared after controlling for other variables in the model. The R-two for this model is 12.7%, a difference of 0.5% from model 1.

In view of the results obtained after the analysis of the net effects, we can comment on the assumptions made at the beginning of this work.

Hypothesis 1: *Preterm births are more prone to low birth weight than full-term births*. This hypothesis is supported. Preterm births are 1.2 times more likely to be born at low birth weight than full-term births.

Hypothesis 2: *Twin pregnancies are more prone to low birth weight than singleton pregnancies.* This hypothesis is also supported. Women who give birth to twin pregnancies are fifteen times more likely to give birth to low birth weight babies.

Hypothesis 3: *Mothers younger than 20 years and those aged 35 years and older are at greater risk for low birth weight than those aged 20-34 years.* Also, this hypothesis is partially supported. The results of the analyses show that mothers under 20 years of age are twice as likely to give birth to low birth weight babies as those between 20 and 34 years of age. It should be noted that the association between low birth weight and age 35 years and older was not tested in the study.

Hypothesis 4: *Women out of union are more prone to low birth weight than those in union.* This hypothesis was not tested.

Hypothesis 5: *Mothers carrying unwanted pregnancies are at greater risk of low birth weight than those carrying wanted pregnancies.* This hypothesis is not tested in this work.

Hypothesis 6: *Women living in unsettled areas are at greater risk of LBW than those living in* *settled areas.* This hypothesis was not tested in this work.

Hypothesis 7: *Having no education is a factor associated with LBW.* This hypothesis is not verified in this work.

Hypothesis 8: *The female sex is more exposed to low weight than the male sex.* This hypothesis is supported. Female children are 1.3 times more likely to be born low birth weight than male children.

Hypothesis 9: *LBW is more common among mothers from low-income households than among those from high-income households.* This hypothesis is not tested in this work.

Hypothesis 10: ***Working*** *for pay is a protective factor against LBW.* This hypothesis is tested.

Hypothesis 11: *Mossi women are more exposed to NPF than other women.* This hypothesis was not tested.

III.5 Discussion of results

The multivariate analysis, in particular the binary logistic regression method, made it possible to determine the gross and net effects of the different explanatory variables on the occurrence of low birth weight in this study. The results of the analysis are discussed taking into account the elements of the Burkinabe context, provided by the literature review.

111.5.1 Statistically present relationships

The results of the study show that the mother's age at delivery remains a factor strongly associated with the occurrence of low birth weight.

Indeed, mothers under 20 years of age at the time of delivery are more likely to give birth to low birth weight babies than those between 20 and 34 years of age. A large number of studies conducted in Africa on low birth weight confirm this result (OUSMANE, 2001). This could be explained by the fact that the physiological development of these young mothers is not at full term at the time of delivery, which also increases the risk of maternal mortality in the same age group. Also, young mothers are those who often have a very low level of education and income, thus limiting their access to prenatal health services and information.

In addition, the study found that twinhood is strongly associated with the occurrence of low birth weight. Women with twin pregnancies are more likely to deliver low birth weight babies than those with singleton pregnancies. This result is consistent with a study conducted in the Tunisian Sahel (LETAIEF, 2001).

This can be explained by the malnutrition of pregnant women, especially considering the peripheral context in which the study took place, where less attention is paid to the quality of food.

Also women with multiple pregnancies are prone to high blood pressure and anemia.

Being born a girl is a factor that predisposes to low birth weight. Most research studies have shown the association of this variable with the occurrence of low birth weight (KABORE *et al.,* 2007; MEDA *et al.,* 1995). KRAMER (1987) justifies this by the susceptibility of girls to intrauterine growth retardation compared to boys in Western countries, which could certainly be valid for Third World countries in general, but especially for the periphery of Ouagadougou, through malnutrition.

This work also found that mothers from the Mossi ethnic group were more likely to give birth to low birth weight babies than other ethnic groups. Although this association was seen only in the raw effects results of the regression, this result seems hardly surprising given that pregnancy beliefs among Mossi women are often the cause of late reporting of their pregnancies, which also explains their late use of prenatal health services. But this could be verified by an in-depth qualitative study in these outlying areas.

Unwanted pregnancies are subject to late reporting and, consequently, late use of prenatal care services. Despite the confounding effect of this variable in this work, these results are consistent with other work (MOUFTAOU, 2011). Unintended pregnancies also lead some women to resort to traditional abortion practices that, when unsuccessful, interfere with the normal intrauterine development of the fetus reflecting its birth weight.

Finally, this study reveals that premature births are more exposed to the risk of low birth weight than those arriving at term. A similar trend has been observed by other authors who indicate a strong association (PAMBOU, 2006).

This is simply because babies who are born prematurely have not completed their intrauterine development.

111.5.2 Absent statistical relationships.

This study shows that the area of residence, marital status, religious affiliation of the mother, level of education, standard of living of the household, and the mother's occupation are not statistically significant in explaining the occurrence of low birth weight.

The results of the study revealed that the mother's level of education was not associated with the occurrence of low birth weight. This result is not consistent with that observed in a study conducted in Cameroon where women who had no education were more likely to give birth to low birth weight babies (TIETCHE, 1998). This may be due to the strong role of the media in these outlying areas.

Indeed, most of the inhabitants of these peripheral areas are from the Mossi ethnic group (91%) and

Mooré is the most widely spoken language of communication in Ouagadougou, but also the language most used by the public and private media to communicate and convey information and messages about health education in general and access to prenatal consultation services in particular by decision-makers and health personnel.

Also, the woman's standard of living was not associated with the occurrence of low birth weight in this work. These results do not corroborate those of Tietche and colleagues who found that a low standard of living for women is a risk factor for low birth weight. These same results were obtained in a study conducted in Benin (AKPOVI, 1998). As explanatory elements, we know that since the adoption of the Bamako Initiative (BI) by the Burkinabe government in 1987, health policies have focused on pregnant women and children, given the alarming morbidity and mortality indicators in these population groups, through a strategy of exemption from health care costs, thus facilitating access to health care for women in these peripheral areas, regardless of their income level. This ease of access to health care facilities for these vulnerable groups has also been reinforced by the efforts of the Burkinabe authorities to achieve the Millennium Development Goals (MDG)[21] 4 and 5. In addition, in 2000, the government of Burkina Faso established a national health policy (PNS), which has allowed progress to be made in improving access to health care and services.

Finally, the residential area is not statistically associated with the occurrence of low birth weight according to the results of the analysis. This could probably be explained by the geographical proximity of the non-housed areas to those housed in areas with primary health care facilities offering prenatal care services, and it could be an imitation effect of women living in non-housed areas in terms of access to care and attendance at prenatal care services.

111.5.3 Limits

The study seeks to contribute to the strengthening of knowledge on the factors associated with low birth weight in the outlying areas of the capital Ouagadougou. However, it has certain limitations that should be highlighted.

The database used in the study does not contain certain key variables, such as the quality of the pregnant woman's diet, which is essential to explain the occurrence of low birth weight, or the prenatal consultation (PC), which was only collected from round 3 onwards. Furthermore, the data in the analysis could be biased by reporting errors (reliability of responses) that would negatively affect the quality of the results.

---

21 MDG 4: Reduce by two-thirds, between 1990 and 2015, the under-five mortality rate. MDG 5: Reduce by three quarters, between 1990 and 2015, the maternal mortality ratio.

CONCLUSION.

The study confirmed that low birth weight remains a reality in the Ouagadougou Population Observatory monitoring areas with a proportion of 13.1%. The determinants statistically associated with this phenomenon were the age of the mothers at delivery, especially when it is less than 20 years old, twin pregnancies, the desirability of pregnancy, prematurity, the sex of the baby and ethnicity.

The results of the analyses show that, in addition to the physiological or genetic determinants that cannot be modified, certain determinants such as the mother's age at delivery and gestational age, particularly preterm births, can be controlled.

This is why well-targeted and coordinated awareness-raising activities on the age of the mother at her first delivery, which often depends on early marriage, and especially on the diet of the pregnant woman, which can be either a protective factor or a factor of exposure to prematurity, could have an impact on the occurrence of low birth weight in these outlying areas.

However, further study of the dietary pattern of pregnant women and especially the attendance at antenatal clinics in these areas monitored by the OPO would be necessary to determine the contribution of these factors to the occurrence of low birth weight.

BIBLIOGRAPHIC REFERENCES

ACC/SCN. (2000). Low birthweight (Nutrition Policy Paper 18). Geneva.

ACC/SCN. (2000) "Fourth report on the world nutrition situation. Geneva.

AKOTO,E. (1993). *Socio-cultural Determinants of Child Mortality in Black Africa: Hypotheses and Explanatory Research.* Louvain: Louvain-La-Neuve Académia.

AKPOVI, J. PERRIN, R .X. ALIHONOU, E. (1998). Risk factors for low birth weight in Cotonou. *Le Benin Medical: Special Gynecology and Obstetrics* (8), 72.

ALBANE, T. (2005). Food behavior of pregnant women in Ouagadougou. *Dissertation D.E.S.S in Nutrition and Food in Developing Countries*. Ouagadougou, Burkina Faso.

ALBERTSSON-WIKLAND, K., KARLBERG J. (1994). Natural growth in children born small for gestational age with and without catch-up growth. *Acta Pediatrica , 399*, 64-70.

ALEGRE,A.; RODRIGUEZ-ESCUDERO, F.J., CRUZ, E., PRADAR,-E. (1984). Influence of work during pregnancy on fetal weight. *Journal of Reproductive Medicine , 5* (29), 334-336.

ANOH, A., FASSASSI, R and VIMARD, P.F. (2002). *Population Policy and Family Planning in Côte d'Ivoire.* Les dossiers du CEPED.

ARMSTRONG, B.G., MACDONALD. A.D., SLOAN M. (1992). Cigarette, alcohol and coffee consumption and spontaneous abortion. *American Journal of Public Health , 82* (1), 85-87.

ASHWORTH, A. (1998). Effects of intrauterine growth retardation on mortality and morbidity in infants and young children. *European Journal of Clinical Nutrition , 52*, 34-42.

AUBRY, P. (2003). Malaria: update. *Obstet.Gynecol ,* 22.

BDMS-ONE. (2010). Birth statistics data. Belgium.

BEHRMAN,R. (1985). *Preventing low birth weight. Summary.* Washington D.C. Division of Health Promotion and Disease Prevention Institute of Medicine, National Academy Press.

BHUTTA, Z.A., DARMSTADT, G.L., HASAN,B. S,. HAWS R, A. (2005). Communitybased interventions for improving perinatal and neonatal health outcomes in developing countries: a review of the evidence. *Pediatrics* (115 (suppl)), S519-S617.

BENINGUISSE, G. (2003), Entre tradition et modernité. Les fondements sociaux de la prise en charge de la grossesse et de l'accouchement au Cameroun, Academia- Bruylant/L'Harmattan, Louvain-la-Neuve, 297.

BOAZ-O N. (1999). Tropical diseases and pregnancy. *19* (2), 56.

BOBOSSI, SG., MBONGO-ZINDAMOYEN,AN., KALAMBAY,K., DIEMER, H., SIOPATHIS, R.M. (1999). Factors of mortality of newborns in Central African semi-rural areas. *Médecine d'Afrique Noire, 46* (10), 446.

BONNET, D. (1988), Corps biologique et corps social. Procreation et maladies de l'enfant en pays mossi, Burkina Faso, Editions l'ORSTOM, Paris, 138.

BOYER, F D. (2009). *Peuplement de Ouagadougou et développement urbain.* Draft, IRD, Ouagadougou.

BRICAIRE, F., DANIS, M., GENTILINI, M. (1993). Malaria and pregnancy. *Cahier de Santé 3,* 289-292.

CALDWELL, J.C. (1979). Education as a factor in mortality decline: an examination of Nigerian data. *Populations Studies , 33* (3), 395-415.

CAMARA, B., DIACK, B., DIOUF, S., SY, H., SALL, M.G., BA, M., SARR, K., HANNE, C., THIAM, L., DIOUF, D., SOW, M., FALL (1996). Low birth weight: Frequency and risk factors in the district of Guediawaye (BANLIEUE DE DAKAR - SENEGAL). *Médecine d'Afrique Noire, 43* (5), 261-265.

CASILLI ,W.G., VALLIN, J. (2002). Demography: analysis and synthesis.The determinants of mortality *3*.

CHAULIAC, M. (1991). Interpretation of anthropometric measurements of the newborn. Synthèse bibliographique. *Les bulletins du Centre International de L'Enfance.* (34).

COLES, C.D. (1993). Impact of prenatal alcohol exposure on the newborn and the child. *Clinical Obstetrics and Gynecology , 36* (2), 255-266.

COLIN, C., DESROSIERS, H. (1989). Naitre égaux et en Santé: Avis sur la grossesse en milieu défavorisé, Quebec. 153.

CONGO, Z. (2007). *Les facteurs de la contraception au Burkina Faso au tournant du siècle.* Les collections du CEPED.

DAVIDSON, N., FELICE, M . (1992). Adolescent pregnancy. In: Friedman S,Fisher M, Schonberg S, eds.Comprehensive adolescent health careSt Louis, MO. *Quality Medical Publishing Inc, ,* 1026-1040.

DE ONIS, M., VILLAR, J., GULMEZOGLU, M. (1998). Nutritional intervention to prevent intra uterine growth retardation: Evidence from randomized controlled trials. *European journal of clinical nutrition , 58* (1), 83-93.

DELPISHCH, A., ATTIA, E., DRAMMOND, S., BRABIN, B.J. (2005). Adolescent smoking in pregnancy and birth outcomes. *European Journal of Public Health, 16* (2), 168172.

E&D.(2011).*Activity Report.*

http://www.enfantsetdeveloppement.org/documentation/Rapports-moraux-8/48-Rapport-   moral-2011.pdf. [accessed May 28, 2013].

ERNHART, C., SOKOL, R.J., MARTIER, S., MORON, P., NADLER, D., AGER, J.W., WOLF, A. (1987). Alcohol teratogenicity in the human: a detailed assessment of the specificity, critical period, and threshold. *American Journal of Obstetrics and Gynecology, 156* (1), 33-39.

EZECHI ,O.C., MAKINDE, O.N., KALU, B.E., NNATU, S.N. (2003). Risk Factors for preterm delivery in South Western Nigeria. *J Obstet Gynaecol, 23* (4), 387-91.

FRIEDL, J. (1982). Mechanisms of interaction between Education and health: Discussion. *Health Policy and Education, 38* (11), 101-104.

GIBBS, R.S., ROMERO, R., HILLIER, S.L., ESCHEMBCH, D.A., SWEET, R.L. (1992). A review of premature birth and subclinical infection. *American Journal of Obstetrics and Gynecology, 5* (166), 1515-1528.

HANVEY ,L. A. (1994). *The health of Canada's children: a profile from the Canadian Institute of Child Health* (ed.). Ottawa,, Ottawa: Canadian Institute of Child Health.

HARRISON ,H.A. (1985). Relationships between maternal height, fetal birth and cephalopelvic disproportion suggest that young Nigerian primigravidae grow during pregnancy. *British Journal of Obstetrics and Gynaecology, 5* (92), 42-48.

HEDEGAARD, M., HENRIKSEN, T.B., SABROE, S., SECHER, N.J. (1993). psychological distress in pregnancy and preterm delivery. *British Medical Journal, 307* (6898), 234-239.

HENRIKSEN, T. S. (1994). Employment during pregnancy in relation to risk factors and pregnancy outcome. *British Journal of Obstetrics and Gynaecology, 10* (101), 858-856.

HINDS, T.S., WEST, W.L., KNIGHT, E.M., HARLAND, B.F. (1996). The effect of caffeine on pregnancy outcome variables. *Nutrition Revue, 54* (7), 203-207.

NATIONAL INSTITUTE OF STATISTICS AND DEMOGRAPHY (2009). Analysis of some results of the data from the main phase of the Integrated Survey on Living Conditions of Households EICVM.

NATIONAL INSTITUTE OF STATISTICS AND DEMOGRAPHY (2009). Monograph of the urban commune of Ouagadougou. Ouagadougou: Burkina Faso.

NATIONAL INSTITUTE OF STATISTICS AND DEMOGRAPHY (2008). *Multiple Indicator Cluster Survey: Suivi de la situation des enfants et des femmes 2006.* Ouagadougou: Burkina Faso.

JACOBSON, J.L., JACOBSON, S.W., SOKOL, R.J., MARTIER, S.S., AGER, J.W., SHANKARAN, S. (1994). Effects of alcohol use, smoking, and illicit drug on fetal growth in black infants. *Journal of pediactrics , 124* (5), 757-764.

JOHNSTONE, F and INGLIS, L. (1974). Familial trends in low birth weight. *British Medical Journal, 3* (5932), 659-661.

KABORE, P., DONNEN, P., WILMET, D. (2007). Obstetrical risk factors for low birth weight at term in rural Sahelian settings. *Revue de* Santé *publique, 19* (6), pp. 189-197.

KAFANDO, Y. (2004). Urban environment and health problems in Ouagadougou: the case of the Cissin district. *Maitrise thesis/Unité de Formation et de Recherche en Sciences Humaines (U.F.R./S.H.).* Ouagadougou, University of Ouagadougou.78p.

KESSEL,.SS. (1988). Racial differences in pregnancy outcomes. *Clin. Perinatol* (15), 745.

KETTERLINUS, R.D., HENDERSON, S.H., LAMB, M.E. (1990). Maternal age,sociodemographics, prenatal health and behavior: influences on neonatal risk status. *Journal of Adolescent Health Care, 11* (5), 423-431.

KOLOGO, O. (2008). *Issues of Franco-Burkinabe decentralized cooperation in urban development.*

http://www.memoireonline.com/05/10/3485/m_Enjeux-cooperation-decentralisee-franco-burkinabe-in-development-urban6.html.[Accessed May 28, 2013].

KOUTON, E. (1992). Evaluation and research on early fertility in Benin. *Cahier de l'IFORD* (3), 121.

KRAMER, K., JOSEPH, K., MARCOUX ,S., OHLSSON, A., WEN, S., ALLEN, A (1998). Determinants of Preterm Birth Rates in Canada from 1981 through 1983 and from 1992 through 1994. *New England Journal of Medicine , 339* (20), 1434-1439.

KRAMER,.M.S. (1987). Determinants of low birth weight: Methodological assessment and meta-analysis. *Bulletin of the World Health Organization , 65* (5), 663-737.

LETAIEF, M., SOLTANI, M.S., BEN SALEM, K., BCHIR, A. (2001). Epidemiology of ponderal insufficiency at birth in the Tunisian Sahel. Santé *Publique , 13* (4), 359366.

LIEBERMAN, E., GREMY, I., LANG ,J.M., COHEN, A.P. (1994). Low birth weight at term and the timing of fetal exposure to maternal smoking. *Amercan Journal of Public Health , 84* (7),

1127-1131.

MAATOUK ,F., BELGACEM, B., BELGACEM, R., GHEDIRA, H.,GEMMALL, B. (1996). Prevalence of dental caries in low birth weight children. *eastern Mediterranean Health Journal , 2* (2).

MABIALA-BABELA, J.R., MATINGOU ,V.C., SENGA, P. (2007). Risk factors for low birth weight in Brazzaville, Congo. *Journal of Gynecology Obstetrics and Reproductive Biology, 36* (8), 795-98.

MACDERMOTT, R.I. (1995). Bacterials vasinosis. *British Journal of Obstetrics and Gynaecology , 2* (102), 92-94.

MARBURY, M.C., LINN, S., MONSON R, SCHOENBAUM S, STUBBLEFIELD P.G, RYAN KJ. (1983). The association of alcohol consumption with outcome of pregnancy. *American Journal of Public Health , 73* (10), 1165-1168.

MARTIN, T.R., BRACKEN, M.B. (1987). The association between low birth weight and caffeine consumption during pregnancy. *American Journal of Epidemiology , 126* (5), 813821.

MATHAI, M., VISAYASRI, R., BABU, S., JEYASEELAN, L. (1992). Passive maternal smoking and birth weight in a south Indian Population. *British Journal of Obstetrics and gynaecology , 99* (4), 342-343.

MATTEELLI, A., CALIGARIS, S., CASTELLI, F. (1997). The placenta and malaria. *Ann.Trop. Med. Parasitol. , 91* (7), 803-810.

MBOUP, G., KODJOGBE, N (1999). Perspectives on family planning and reproductive health in Benin. *National Institute of Statistics and Economic Analysis and Macro International Inc, Calverton , 97.*

HYPERLINK

"http://www.refdoc.fr/?traduire=en&FormRechercher=submit&FormRechercher_Txt_Recher che_name_attr=authorsName:%20%28MEDA%29"	**MEDA,	N.	,	HYPERLINK** "http://www.refdoc.fr/?traduire=en&FormRechercher=submit&FormRechercher_Txt_Recher che_name_attr=authorsName:%20%28SOULA%29"	**SOULA,	G.	HYPERLINK** "http://www.refdoc.fr/?traduire=en&FormRechercher=submit&FormRechercher_Txt_Recher che_name_attr=authorsName:%20%28DABIS%29"	**DABIS,	F.	,	HYPERLINK** "http://www.refdoc.fr/?translate=en&FormSearch=submit&FormSearch_Txt_Reach che_name_attr=authorsName:%20%28COUSENS%29"	**COUSENS,	S.	,	HYPERLINK** "http://www.refdoc.fr/?traduire=en&FormRechercher=submit&FormRechercher_Txt_Recher

che_name_attr=authorsName:%20%28SOME%29" **SOME, A. ,** HYPERLINK "http://www.refdoc.fr/?translate=en&FormRecher=submit&FormRecher_Txt_Recher che_name_attr=authorsName:%20%28MERTENS%29" **MERTENS, T. ,** HYPERLINK "http://www.refdoc.fr/?traduire=en&FormRechercher=submit&FormRechercher_Txt_Recher che_name_attr=authorsName:%20%28SALAMON%29" **SALAMON, R.** (1995). Risk factors for prematurity and intrauterine growth retardation in Burkina Faso. HYPERLINK "http://www.refdoc.fr/?traduire=en&FormRechercher=submit&FormRechercher_Txt_Recher che_name_attr=listeTitreSerie:%20%28Revue%20d%27%C3%A9pid%C3%A9miologie%20 et%20de%20sant%C3%A9%20publique%29" Revue d'épidémiologie et de santé publique . vol. 43, n° 3, pp. 215-224.

MILLAR ,W., WADHERA, W., NIMROD, C . (1990). *Multiple births: Trends and behaviors in Canada.* Health Report.

MILLS, J.L., GRAUBARD ,B.I., HARLEY, E.E., RHOADS, G.G., BERENDES, H.W. (1984). Maternal alcohol consumption and birth weight. How much drinking during pregnancy is safe? *Journal of the American Medical association , 252* (14), 1875-1879.

MRC/RCOG. (1988). Interim report of the Medical Research Council/Royal College of obstetricians and Gynaecologists multicentre randomized trial of cervical cerclage. *British Journal of Obstetrics and Gynaecology , 5* (95), 437-445.

NCHS. (1981). Basic data on anthropometric measurements and angular measurements of the hip and knee joints for selected age groups 1-74 years. *Hyattsville.*

NKURUNZIZA, E., KANYANA, A (2008). Influence of maternal age and parity on birth weight at Ngozi Hospital from 2001 to 2003. *Médecine d'Afrique Noire* (5510), 537-541.

NORDENTOFT, M., LOU, H.C., HANSEN, D., NIM, J., PRYDA, O., RUBIN, P.,HEMMINGSEN, R. (1996). Intrauterine growth retardation and premature delivery: the influence of maternal smoking and psychosocial factors. *American Journal of Public Health , 86* (3), 347-354.

OAKLEYA,. R. (1990). Social support and pregnancy outcome. *British Journal of Obstetrics and Gynaecology , 2* (97), 155-162.

OHLSSON, A., SHAH, P (2008). Determinants and prevention of low birth weight: A synopsis of the evidence. *Institute of health economics, Alberta Canada , 274.*

WHO. (2012). *Coming too soon: a report of global efforts addressing preterm births.* New York.

WHO. (2003). *Lives at risk: Malaria in pregnancy.*

WHO. (1981). Development of indicators for monitoring progress towards health for all by the year 2000. p102.

WHO. (2002). *World Health Report.* New York.

WHO. (1994). *One in five children is born too small, updated data provided by UNICEF field office.* New York.

WHO. (1995). *Use and interpretation of anthropometry. Report of an expert committee, WHO.* Switzerland: Geneva.

OUAGADOUGOU POPULATION OBSERVATORY. (2008). A study site providing up-to-date information and empirical evidence to policymakers. *www.*issp.bf

OUAGADOUGOU POPULATION OBSERVATORY. (2009). *Action-research platform for a better control of urbanization. www.*issp.bf

OSBORN, J.A., HARRIS, S.R., WEINBERG, J. (1993). Fetal alcohol syndrome: review of the literature with the implications for physical therapist. *Physical Therapy, 73* (9), 599-607.

OUEDRAOGO, C. (1994). Education de la mère et soins aux enfants à Ouagadougou. *Les dossiers du CEPED* (27), 37.

OUEDRAOGO, N.L. (2005, July 8). Risk factors associated with intrauterine growth retardation: A case-control study in the city of Ouagadougou. *Final thesis in public* health *and* health *management.* Ouagadougou, Burkina Faso.

OUSMANE, N., DIALLO ,D., DIEGNE, I., MOREAU ,C.J., DIADHIOU, F., KUAKUVI, N. (2001). Maternal risk factors and low birth weight in Senegalese adolescents: the example of a hospital in Dakar. *Cahier d'études et de recherches* francophone/Santé *, 11* (4), 241-4.

PAMBOU, O., NTSIKA-KAYA, P., EKOUNDZOLA, J.R., MAYANDA, F. (2006). Preterm birth at the University Hospital of Brazzaville. *Cahier d'études et de recherches* francophone/santé *, 16* (3), 185-9.

PANETH, NIGEL, S. (1995). The problem of low birth weght. *The future of children , 5* (1), 19-34.

PAPERNIK, E., KEITH, L. (1990). The cost effectiveness of preventing preterm delivery in twin pregnancies. *Acta Geneticae Medicae and Gemellologiae* (39), 361-369.

PARKER, J.D., SCHOENDORF, K.C. (2001). A comparison of recent trends in infant mortality among twins and singletons. *Paediatric and Perinatal Epidemiology* (15), 12-18.

PRADA, J.A., TSANG, R.C. (1998). Biological mechanisms of environmentally induced causes of

IUGR. *European Journal of Clinical Nutrition* (52), 21-28.

RI, MACDERMOTT. (1995). Bacterials vaginosis. *British Journal of Obstetrics and Gynaecology, 102* (2), 92-94.

RIZVI, S., HATCHER, J., JEHAN, L., QURECHI, R. (2007). Meternal risk factors associated with low-birth weight in karachi: a case-control study. *revue de santé de la* mediterranée *orientale , 13* (6), 1344.

ROSSIER, C., SOURA, A., LANKOANDE, B., MILLOGO, M. (2011). *Ouagadougou Population Observatory: Data* collected *in round 0, round 1 and round 2: Descriptive report.* Descriptive, Institut Supérieur des Sciences de la Population.www.issp.bf/OPO, Ouagadougou.

SCOTT, K., USHER, R. (1996). Tetal Malnutrition: it's incidence causes. *Am.J.Obstet.Gynecol, 94* (8), 951-963.

SHAH, P., OHLSSON, A. (2002). Literature review of low birth weight, including small for gestation age and preterm birth. *Toronto public health* , 131.

SHETTY, P.S., JAMES, W.P.T. (1994). Body Mass Index: A Measure of Chronic Energy Deficiency in Adults. *Food and Nutrition Paper* (56).

SHIONO, H.P., KLEBANOFF, M.A., GRAUBARD, B.I., BERENDES, H.W., RHOADS, G.G. (1986). Birth weight among women of different ethnic groups. *Am. J. Public Health , 3* (1), 48-52.

SHIONO, P & PATRICIA, I. (1995). Low birth weght:analysis and recommendations. *The future of children , 5* (1), 1-18.

SHULMAN, C.E. (1999). Malaria in pregnancy: its relevance to safe motherhood programmes. *Ann. Trop. Med. Parasitol. , 93*, 59-66.

SIMPSON, J. (1993). Are physical activity and employment related to preterm birth and low birth weight? *American Journal of Obstetrics and Gynecology , 4* (168), 1231-1238.

STARFIELD, B., SHAPIRO, S., WEISS, J., LIANG, KY., RA K, PAIGE, D., WANG, XB. (1991). Race, family income and low birthweight. *Am. J. Epidemiol. , 134* (10), 1167-74.

STEKETEE, R.W., WIRIMA, J.J., SLUTSKER, L ., HEYMANN, D.L., BREMAN, J.G. (1996). The problem of malaria and malaria control in pregnancy in sub-Saharan Africa. *American Journal of Tropical medicine and Hygiene, 55* (1), 2-7.

STEKETEE, R.W. (2003). Pregnancy, nutrition and parasitic diseases. *J. Nutr. , 133*, 16611667.

STOLTZFUS, R.J. (1997). Hookworm control as a strategy to prevent iron deficiency. *Nutrition Reviews , 55* (6), 223-232.

STROMLAND, K., HELLSTROM, A. (1996). Fetal alcohol syndrome: an ophthalmological and socioeducational prospective study. *Pediatrics , 97* (6), 845-850.

TIETCHE, H., GOUFACK ,G., KAGO, I., MBONDA, E., KOKI NDOMBO ,P.O., LEKE, R.I. (1998). Etiological factors associated with intrauterine growth retardation in Yaounde (Cameroon): A preliminary study. *Médecine d'Afrique Noire, 6,* 45.

UNICEF. (2004). *Low Birthweight: Country, regional and global estimates.* New York.

VIRJI,S.K. (1991). The relationship between alcohol consumption during pregnancy and infant birth weight. An epidemiologic study. *Acta Obstetricia et gynecolgica scandinavica , 70* (4-5), 303-308.

WHO. (1979). Definitions and recommendations, International statistical classification of diseases, *1.* Geneva.

WHO. (1997). National reports on the third evaluation of the implementation of "Health for All" strategies. *WHO Global Database, New Delhi.*

WHO/UNICEF. (2003). *Africa Malaria Report.* Geneva: WHO New-York.

ZEITLIN, J., WILDMAN, K., BREART, G., BLONDEL, B. (2003). PERISTAT study: indicators for monitoring and evaluating perinatal health.